Wonderful things from 400 years of collecting:

The Bodleian Library
1602 - 2002

Wonderful things from 400 years of collecting:

The Bodleian Library
1602-2002

An exhibition to mark the quatercentenary of the Bodleian
July to December 2002

BODLEIAN LIBRARY
UNIVERSITY OF OXFORD

First published in 2002 by the Bodleian Library, Broad Street, Oxford OX1 3BG
Reprinted in 2011
www.bodleianbookshop.co.uk

ISBN 978-1-85124-077-7
This edition © Bodleian Library, University of Oxford, 2002

Catalogue designed and typeset in Adobe Caslon by Dot Little at the Bodleian Library
Printed and bound by Great Wall Printing, China

Inside cover illustration from item 30 Bernhard von Breydenbach, *Peregrinatio in terram sanctam*.
Title page illustration from item 25 Gaius Plinius Secundus, *Historia naturalis*, trans. Cristoforo Landino.

Contents

Preface

'Wonderful things' was Howard Carter's famous description of what he saw when he first glimpsed the treasures of Tutankhamun's tomb in 1922. This exhibition, the second celebrating the Bodleian Library's quatercentenary, complements the first, *Sir Thomas Bodley and his library*, which told the story of the refoundation of the University's library and its establishment as a successful academic institution, by showing the growth of its collections thereafter. These collections have, over the years, turned the library into a research resource of national and international importance. The three principal ways of acquisition are by gift, purchase, and legal deposit. In the 17th and 18th centuries donations were the most important additions; as the 19th century progressed the copyright privilege, developed in a series of acts from Sir Thomas's agreement with the Stationers' Company in 1610/11, gave the Library books and periodicals on a scale hitherto undreamt of; and, from the earliest days, collections and individual items have been bought. The Library's finances have always been limited, but outside help has often been called upon, as in the case of the recent purchase of the important Mendelssohn manuscript exhibited (item 35). The 'wonderful things' here have been chosen to show the extent, variety, and quality of the Library's holdings and how these holdings were gathered in.

Acknowledgements

We should like to thank all the staff who have contributed to the selection and description of items from their collections; the photographers Jackie Merralls and Nick Cistone for providing the illustrations in this catalogue; the conservators Dana Josephson and Robert Minte for preparing the material for display; and Dot Little for designing the catalogue. Items 8 and 74 are reproduced by kind permission of the Tolkien Estate; Leonard Baskin's woodcut from item 14 is reproduced by kind permission of Lisa Baskin and the Gehenna Press.

English literature

1-8

I The First Folio

Mr. William Shakespeares Comedies, histories, & tragedies. Published according to the true originall copies. London, printed by Isaac Jaggard, and Ed. Blount, 1623.

This copy of what was to become the most important book in the English language was delivered to the Bodleian Library in sheets in late 1623 under the terms of Sir Thomas Bodley's arrangement with the Stationers' Company in 1610. (The agreement, confirmed in 1612, that members of the Company should deposit a perfect copy of every book they printed was later incorporated into the various copyright acts, all affirming the Library's status as a copyright library.) The sheets were sent out to be bound by a local binder early in 1624, assigned a shelfmark and chained to a shelf in Arts End, and duly appeared in the 1635 *Appendix* to the printed catalogue. However, it was not present in the next catalogue (1674) and it is assumed that it was disposed of when the Third Folio was received in 1664. With its seven additional plays it would have superseded (in contemporary eyes) the First Folio, which perhaps then became one of the 'superfluous Library Books sold by order of the Curators' to Richard Davis the Oxford bookseller for £24.

In 1905 Gladwin Turbutt, a Magdalen College graduate, brought to the Library a badly worn copy of the First Folio seeking advice as to what should be done to it. It belonged to his father and was part of the library of Ogston Hall, Derbyshire; it is thought it had been acquired in the second quarter of the eighteenth century by Richard Turbutt, a known collector of English drama. The volume was shown to Strickland Gibson, a young assistant librarian who had a special interest in Oxford binding; he immediately recognized the brown calf binding as Oxford work; and the upper board was damaged in a way which suggested that the metal clip to which a chain had been attached had been roughly pulled off: evidence for the possibility that this was the original Bodleian copy. What clinched the identification was the printed waste paper used by the binder to line the boards. The First Folio sheets had been sent to the binder William Wildgoose on 17 February 1624 with those of seven other books; three of these and the Shakespeare have linings from the same book, an edition of Cicero printed by Pafraet in Deventer in the early 1480s.

During the forty years that the First Folio was chained to its shelf in the Library's Arts End it was heavily used, presumably by young graduate students of the University (men only, of course, and BAs because undergraduates were not allowed to read in the Library). Much was made in 1905 of the evidence which the wear to the pages provided for the relative admiration of each of the plays. *Romeo and Juliet* was judged most read, and the most worn page of all contains the end of the balcony scene; next was *Julius Caesar*, then *The Tempest*; least read were *King John* and *Richard II*.

The Bodleian was determined to buy back this very special copy of Shakespeare's plays and proposed to Turbutt to do so by subscriptions from past and present members of the University. A value had not then been put upon the book. In October 1905 Turbutt reported that he had received an offer of £3000 (a very high price reflecting the unique status of this copy from, it later became known, Henry C. Folger, the American millionaire, who was to amass the largest number of First Folios in the world), and would let the Bodleian have it for this sum if it could be raised within a month, an impossible time limit subsequently extended to 31 March 1906. The appeal was launched (the Bodleian had no funds of its own for anything of this magnitude, and the most it had ever paid for a book was £220 10s for a volume of Anglo-Saxon and other early English charters). By 12 March only £1300 had been raised and E.W.B. Nicholson, Bodley's Librarian, wrote to *The Times* begging for contributions from any source: 'That after two and a half centuries we should have the extraordinary chance of recovering this volume, and should lose it because a single American can spare more money than all Oxford's sons or friends who have been helping us, is a bitter prospect. It is the more bitter because the abnormal value put on this copy by our competitor rests on knowledge ultimately derived from our own staff and our own registers. But from so cruel a gibe of fortune this appeal may perhaps yet save us.' And indeed it did. On 29 March the then shortfall of £500 was given by Lord Strathcona.

Presented by the Stationers' Company, 1623; purchased by subscription, 1906. *Arch. G c.7*

F. Madan, G.M.R. Turbutt, S. Gibson, *The original Bodleian copy of the First Folio of Shakespeare (the Turbutt Shakespeare)*. Oxford, Clarendon Press, 1905.

Mr. WILLIAM
SHAKESPEARES

COMEDIES,
HISTORIES, &
TRAGEDIES.

Published according to the True Originall Copies.

2   John Donne, 'to the Honourable lady, the lady Carew' [1611/12]

More transcriptions were made of John Donne's poems than of any other English poet of the sixteenth and seventeenth centuries, but apart from Latin verse inscriptions in two printed books, the only extant poem by Donne in his own handwriting is the verse epistle printed posthumously in 1633 under the title 'A Letter to the Lady Cary, and Mrs Essex Riche, from Amyens' in the first edition of *Poems, by J. D.* The young women whom the poem celebrates and flatters were daughters of Sir Robert Rich and his second wife, Penelope Devereux

(Philip Sidney's 'Stella'). They were personally unknown to the poet and subsequent rumours of Lady Carey's bearing an illegitimate daughter cast an ironic light on Donne's praise of her saintly 'virtu'.

The manuscript of the poem was found and identified among the family papers of the Duke of Manchester in 1970. It was bought by the Bodleian in the same year.

Purchased, 1970. *MS. Eng. poet. d. 197*

Hence comes yt that yor Beauty wounds not harts
As others, wth prophane and senseall darts,
But as an Influence vertuous thought yt imparts.
But if such frends by the honor of yor sight
Grow capable of thys so great a light,
As to partake yor vertues, and theyr might,
what must I thinke that Influence must doe
when yt finds Sympathy, and Matter too,
vertu and beauty, of the same stuffe, as yow.
wch ys yor noble worthy Sister, shee,
Of whom if what in thys my extasy I see,
And Reuelation of yor both, I see,
I should write here, As in short Galleryes,
The Master at the end large glasses Eyes,
So to present the roome twice to or eyes,
So I should giue thys letter lingth, and say
That wch I playd of yow there ys no way
from eyther, but by th'other, not to stray,
may therfore thys bee 'mough to testify
my true Deuotion, free from flattery,
He that beleeues himselfe, doth never ly.

To the Honourable Lady
the Lady Carew.

Madame
Here where by all all Saints invoked are,
Twere too much scisme to bee singulare,
And gainst a practise generall to warr,
yett turninge to Saints, should my Humilitee
To other Saint then yow directed bee
That were to make my Scisme Heresee:
nor would I bee a Convertite so cold,
As not to tell yit, If thys bee to bold,
Pardons are in thys markett cheaply sold:
when because fayth ys in too low degree,
I thought yt some Apostleship in mee
To speak things wch by fayth alone I see:
That ys, of yow, who are a firmament
Of vertues, where no one ys growen nor spent,
Thay' are yor Materealls, not yor Ornament
Others, whom wee call vertuous, are not so
In theyr whole Substance, but theyr vertues grow
But in theyr Humors, and at Seasons show.
For when through tastles flatt Humilitee
In Dowbakt men some Harmelessnes wee see,
Tis but hys Inglegunie that's vertuous and not hee:
So ys the Blood sometymes, whoeuer ran
To danger vnimportun'd, hee was than
no better then a Sanguine vertuous man.
So Cloystrall Men who in pretence of feare
All Contributions to thys Lyfe forbeare,
Haue vertu in Melancholy, and onely there.
Spirituall Cholerique Critiqs, wch in all
Religious find faults, and forgiue no fall,
Haue through thys Zeale vertu, but in theyr Gall.
wee' are thus but parcell-gilt, To Gold wee are growen,
when vertu ys our Soules Complexione,
who knowes hys vertues Name, or place, hath none.
vertu ys but Aguishe when tis Seuerall,
By' Occasion wak'd, and Circumstantiall:
True vertu ys Soule, allwayes in all deeds all.
Thys vertu, thinkinge to giue Dignitee
To yor Soule found there no Infirmitee,
for yor Soule was as good vertu as shee:
shee therfore wrought vpon that part of yow
wch ys scarse lesse then Soule, as shee could doe,
And soe hath made yor Beauty vertu too;

3 'O Faustus, lay that damned booke aside.'

Christopher Marlowe, *The tragicall history of D. Faustus. As it hath bene acted by the right honorable the Earle of Nottingham his servants*. London, printed by V. S. for Thomas Bushell, 1604.

Marlowe's tragedy was entered in the Stationers' Register by Thomas Bushell in January 1601, over seven years after the playwright's death in mysterious circumstances in 1593. It was in the repertory of the Earl of Nottingham's company from 1594 to 1597, and it is thought that this version formed the basis of the text published by Bushell in 1604. This edition, known as the A text, was reprinted in 1609 and 1611. Meanwhile, in 1602, the Lord Admiral's Men (i.e. the Earl of Nottingham's servants) decided to revive the play, and in order to make it more attractive to a new audience commissioned William Birde and Samuel Rowley to provide additional matter. This longer version, the B text, doesn't appear in print until 1616, after which it became the standard text. All copies of early editions are rare, and the two most important textually, the 1604 and the 1616, survive in single copies. It is not unreasonable to assume that other editions of each version, possibly earlier than those now known, once existed. Critical opinion in the late twentieth century restored the Bodleian copy's textual supremacy after some decades of being treated as a mere memorial reconstruction.

This unique witness to what was probably Marlowe's last play was part of the collection of Edmond Malone (1741–1812), one of the greatest editors of Shakespeare's works. He realized the importance of the first and early editions of Elizabethan and Jacobean plays in establishing their texts, using their evidence to make sense of seeming nonsense, rather than simply improving subjectively as some earlier editors had done. To this end he built one of the largest collections of early English drama and poetry, the Shakespeare holdings being, in Malone's words: 'perhaps the most complete Assemblage of the early editions of his productions that has ever been made'. At his death his books and papers were inherited by his brother Richard, Lord Sunderlin. He passed them to James Boswell, who had been working with Malone on a new variorum edition of Shakespeare, and who undertook to complete the task. This he did in 1821. They were then presented to the Bodleian by Lord Sunderlin, and immediately the Library became the most important repository of early English literature, remaining so until the British Museum began collecting seriously in this field and the great American collections were begun in the late 19th century. With Malone's books the Bodleian had once again a Shakespeare First Folio (see item 1), the unique 1594 *Venus and Adonis* and the unique 1604 *Dr Faustus*.

Presented, 1821. *Mal. 233(3)*

Christopher Marlowe, *The complete works. Vol. II, Dr Faustus*. Edited by Roma Gill. Oxford, Clarendon Press, 1990.

Peter Martin, *Edmond Malone Shakespearean scholar, a literary biography*. Cambridge University Press, 1995.

THE
TRAGICALL

History of D. Faustus.

As it hath bene Acted by the Right
Honorable the Earle of Nottingham his seruants.

Written by Ch. Marl.

LONDON

Printed by V. S. for Thomas Bushell. 1604.

4   'A *little Learning* is a dang'rous Thing: Drink deep, or taste not the *Pierian* Spring:'

Alexander Pope, *An essay on criticism*. Written in the year 1709. Autograph manuscript.

The most striking aspect of this manuscript is its superb imitation of print. It was certainly made with the printer in mind, and Pope clearly wanted there to be no doubt as to how his first separately published poem was to be presented. Pope was a poet who was forever improving his work, usually to brilliant effect. This manuscript of *An essay on criticism* is a fair copy written to show his closest friends as well as to serve as copy for the printer. The print-like characteristics of the opening page, the large capital letters, the underlining to indicate italic type, the catchword at the foot of the page, are emphasized later in the poem with marginal brackets beside triplets and footnotes in a smaller hand which distinguishes between roman and italic without the use of underlining. There are several places where Pope has scratched away the original reading and replaced it with new text, and although the manuscript represents a fairly finished state there are many examples of him revising. Many more changes were made to the published version of 1711, including the omission of a number of lines. Pope kept the manuscript for future reference. The deleted annotations at the top of the first page refer to the poem's

appearance in the 1736 edition of his collected works, a feature of which was the addition of variant readings from earlier editions and manuscripts: 'Insert in ye Head of Alt[erations] whatever verses in this poem are […] as omitted in all ye printed Editions'.

The manuscript was bought at the sale of General William Nassau Lees on 30 July 1889 (lot 77) for £20 10s. (It was one of six lots of Pope's autograph manuscripts from the library of Dr. Charles Chauncey. The Bodleian put bids on all of them but succeeded in buying only this one.) This was a time when English studies were beginning to be taken seriously in Oxford (the Merton professorship of English language and literature had been established in 1882) and no doubt pressure to acquire the manuscripts of one of the great English poets came from this burgeoning interest and the prospect of future research.

Purchased, 1889. *MS. Eng. poet. c.1, fol. 2r*

Robert M. Schmitz, *Pope's Essay on criticism, 1709. A study of the Bodleian manuscript text with facsimiles, transcripts, and variants*. Washington University Press, St Louis, 1962.

Alexander Pope, *An essay on criticism, 1711*. A Scolar Press facsimile. [With a Note by D.F. Foxon.] Menston, 1970.

AN
ESSAY
ON
CRITICISM.

—— Si quid novisti rectius istis.
Candidus imperti; si non, his utere mecum.

'TIS hard to say, if greater Want of Skill
Appear in Writing or in Judging ill;
But, of the two, less dang'rous is th' Offence,
To tire our Patience, than mislead our Sense:
Some few in that, but Numbers err in this,
Ten censure wrong for one who writes amiss;
A Fool might once himself alone expose,
Now One in Verse makes many more in Prose.

   'Tis with our Judgments as our Watches, none
Go just alike, yet each believes his own.
In Poets as true Genius is but rare,
True Taste as seldome is the Critick's share;
Both must alike from Heav'n derive their Light,
These born to judge, as well as those to write.

Let

5   Jane Austen, *Volume the first*, [1793]

Although her first novel, *Sense and sensibility*, was not published until 1811, when its author was thirty-six years old, Jane Austen had begun writing when she was still a child. Brought up in a prosperous country rectory with six brothers and sisters, her literary talents were quickly recognized and encouraged by her father, the Rev. George Austen. The original drafts of these juvenile compositions do not survive, but in 1793 Austen made transcripts of twenty-seven of them, which she collected into three notebooks. *Volume the first* contains some of her earliest fiction, written between the ages of twelve and fifteen. Parodic in nature, the stories display a precocious grasp of literary technique and the popular genres of the day. *Jack & Alice* is a satire on the Gothic novel—'The Johnsons were a family of Love, & though a little addicted to the Bottle & the Dice, had many good Qualities'—a subject to which Austen returned in 1798, in *Northanger Abbey*. The story is 'respectfully inscribed' to her favourite brother 'Francis William Austen Esqr Midshipman on board his Majesty's Ship the Perseverence by his obedient humble Servant The Author'. Francis, like his youngest brother, Charles, eventually rose to the rank of Admiral in the Royal Navy. Cassandra Austen, Jane's older sister, has written on a slip of paper pasted to the endpaper of the volume, 'For my Brother Charles. I think I recollect that a few of the trifles in this vol: were written expressly for his amusement. C.E.A.'

Volume the first was edited by R.W. Chapman in 1933, the same year in which the manuscript was bought, via Chapman, from Mr. H. Deacon and given to the Library by the Friends of the Bodleian. An interesting footnote to the history of English studies at Oxford is the date of acquisition of first editions of Austen's novels by the Bodleian: *Pride and prejudice*, purchased 1921, *Sense and sensibility*, *Emma*, and *Northanger Abbey* and *Persuasion* bought from Chapman in 1922, and *Mansfield Park* from Mr. Justice Mackinnon in 1925.

Presented by the Friends of the Bodleian, 1933. *MS. Don. e. 7, p. 22*

227

Jack & Alice

a novel.

Is respectfully inscribed to Francis William Austen Esq.r Midshipman on board his Majesty's ship the Perseverance by his obedient humble Servant The Author

Chapter the first

Mr Johnson was once up on a time about 53; in a twelvemonth afterwards he was 54, which so much delighted him that he was determined to celebrate his next Birth day by giving a Masquerade to his Children & Freinds. Accordingly on the Day he attained his 55.th year tickets were dispatched to all his Neighbours to that purpose. His acquaintance indeed in that part of the World were not very numerous as they consisted only of Lady

6 Kenneth Grahame, *The Wind in the willows*, 'My dearest Mouse,' 1907

In 1904 Kenneth Grahame was Secretary of the Bank of England when he began telling his four-year-old son Alastair (nicknamed 'Mouse') a birthday story about moles, giraffes, and water-rats. The giraffes, it seems, were quickly forgotten, but over the next three years Grahame's bestiary expanded to include a badger and a toad. When Kenneth and Elsbeth Grahame visited Cornwall in 1907, Alastair—whose often violent and uncontrollable rages belied his nickname—was only persuaded to stay with his governess by the promise that the adventures of Toad would be sent to him through the post in the form of letters. It was these letters, addressed to 'My dearest Mouse', that formed the basis of *The Wind in the willows*, which Grahame published in October 1908, having changed the title from 'The Wind in the reeds' because of its resemblance to Yeats's 'The Wind among the reeds'. Although it received generally poor reviews, it was an immediate popular success and became an international best seller after its publication in America, when President Theodore Roosevelt personally recommended the book to Charles Scribner.

After a troubled childhood and adolescence, Alastair Grahame was found dead on the railway track in Port Meadow during his second year as an undergraduate at Oxford, on 7 May 1920. The Grahames had no other children and when Kenneth Grahame died in 1932 he bequeathed the copyrights in all his works 'to the University of Oxford for the benefit of the Bodleian Library'. Thanks to this bequest, the Bodleian was able to establish a fund for the purchase of books and manuscripts, which would otherwise have been beyond the budget of the Library to acquire. The 'My dearest Mouse' letters and the manuscript of *The Wind in the willows* were presented to the Bodleian by Mrs Elsbeth Grahame in 1943.

In this letter Grahame describes the cross-dressed Toad's escape from prison in a train, with armed police in hot pursuit. 'I am not the washerwoman I seem to be! I am a toad—the well-known Mr. Toad, of Toad Hall …'

Presented, 1943. *MS. Eng. misc. d. 281, fols. 7v–8r*

7a28

TELEPHONE 0197.

The FOWEY HOTEL

FOWEY, CORNWALL, 31st May 1907.

My dearest Mouse

      I hope you are quite well.
I am very glad to hear that you have
been having some boating, and sea-trips
to America & other distant lands.
Now you may like to hear something
further about poor toad. When Toad
heard that they were being pursued
by an engine full of policemen with
revolvers, he fell on his knees among
the coals & cried out "O kind Mr.
Engine-driver, save me, save me, & I
will confess everything! I am not

the washerwoman I seem to be! I am a
toad — the well-known Mr. Toad, of Toad
Hall — & I have escaped from prison, &
those policemen are coming to re-capture
me!" Then the engine-driver looked very
grave, & said — what were you in prison
for, toad?" And the toad blushed
deeply & said — I only borrowed a motor-
car while the people were having lunch.
I didn't mean to steal it really."
"Well", said the engine-driver. "you
have evidently been a bad toad. But
I will save you if I can." So he piled
more coals on the fire, & the engine
flew over the rails; but the engine
behind kept gaining & gaining, &
presently the engine-driver said with
a sigh "I'm afraid its no use. They
must catch us up soon, & then they
will climb along our train till they
get to our engine, & if we attempt to
resist they will shoot us dead with
their revolvers." Then the toad said "O
dear kind Mr. Engine-driver, do think of
something to save me!" And the engine-driver

7 'usylessly unreadable Blue Book of Eccles'

James Joyce, *Ulysses*. Published for the Egoist Press, London, by John Rodker, Paris (Printed by Maurice Darantiere at Dijon, France), 1922.

The most important 20th-century literary text in English had a difficult start in print because of its perceived obscenity. Harriet Shaw Weaver, editor of *The Egoist*, wanted to publish it serially in her magazine in 1918 but couldn't find a printer who would take the risk of prosecution. Ezra Pound, European editor of the Chicago *The Little review*, persuaded the editors to publish his censored version in instalments beginning in March 1918. The United States' Postal Authorities refused to mail some instalments, which were confiscated and burned, and publication ceased after the last issue of 1920 when the magazine's editors were found guilty of publishing obscenity. (Meanwhile *The Egoist* printed five extracts during 1919 and no more.) The obscenity verdict meant that any further publication in the English-speaking world would risk falling foul of the law. But Joyce moved to Paris in July 1920 where he soon met Sylvia Beach, owner of the Shakespeare and Company bookshop and keen promoter of new writing. She offered to have *Ulysses* printed by Maurice Darantiere in Dijon and publish it with her bookshop's name as imprint, her costs to be met by advance subscription. Joyce accepted and on 2 February 1922, his 40th birthday, *Ulysses* was published in Paris; the print run was 1000 numbered copies. Harriet Weaver and John Rodker, a poet and printer living in Paris, were keen to publish an English edition. Darantiere printed for the Egoist Press another 2000 numbered copies (500 of which were burned by the New York postal

authorities), and a few unnumbered, one of which was deposited in the Bodleian Library under the terms of the copyright act. Publication day was 12 October; the Library received this copy in December. It was placed with the pornography, and referenced Φ d. 127. It wasn't until 1936 that the text became freely available in this country when it was published by John Lane The Bodley Head, in a format similar to the Darantiere edition and with the famous Eric Gill bow stamped in gilt on its green cover.

In 2001 the Bodleian was bequeathed John Ryder's papers and a selection of his books. He was for many years designer for Bodley Head, and was notably responsible for what is arguably the most readable edition of *Ulysses*, the small format Bodley Head edition of 1960. With his books came a rich collection of editions of this classic novel, though without a copy of the first Darantiere printing; however the Bodleian had already bought a copy of this, no. 785, in 1964.

Joyce referred to *Ulysses* in *Finnegans wake* as his 'usylessly unreadable Blue Book of Eccles', recalling the blue paper wrappers in which the first French printings were issued.

Legal deposit, 1922.   *Arch. AA d.198*

James Joyce, *Ulysses*. Edited with an introduction and notes by Jeri Johnson. Oxford World's Classics, Oxford University Press, 1998.

John Ryder, 'Editing *Ulysses* typographically' in *Scholarly publishing*, 18/2 (1987), 108–24.

ULYSSES

BY

JAMES JOYCE

8   J.R.R. Tolkien, *The Two towers*, 'Shelob's Lair'

During the twelve years that he spent writing *The Lord of the rings* Tolkien made a series of sketches, maps and elaborate drawings to accompany the story, extracts of which he read to C.S. Lewis, Charles Williams and other members of the Oxford group, the Inklings, an informal gathering of socially and aesthetically conservative, Christian academics and their friends, who met regularly in Lewis's rooms in Magdalen College. Here, in a congenial, all-male atmosphere of 'beer and baccy', they discussed works in progress and the Anglo-Saxon Heroic literature they admired. Lewis read the opening of *The Lion, the Witch and the Wardrobe* to Tolkien in 1949, who was said to dislike it intensely, but when *The Fellowship of the ring* was published on 29 July 1954, Lewis reviewed the novel in glowing terms in *Time & Tide* and also contributed a eulogistic blurb for the dust-jacket, in which he praised its 'heroic seriousness' and 'endless diversity of scenes and characters—comic, epic, monstrous, or diabolic!'

This page is from an early draft of the closing scenes of *The Two towers*, where Frodo and Sam are attempting to cross into Mordor through the pass of Kirith [Cirith] Ungol. At this stage in the evolution of the narrative the giant spider who attacks and paralyses Frodo is called Ungoliant rather than Shelob. Tolkien added the title 'Shelob's Lair' to his pencil, ink and crayon sketch at a later date.

This single manuscript leaf, together with other examples of Tolkien's art-work, was given to the Bodleian by the trustees of Tolkien's estate, after having been exhibited at the Ashmolean Museum in 1977. The complete manuscript of *The Lord of the rings* is at Marquette University, Milwaukee.

Presented, 1977. *MS. Tolkien drawings 81*

'That's that!' said Sam. 'What we expected. But I don't like it. I suppose we've no just exactly where he wanted to bring us. Well, let's get moving away as quick as we can. That has the aches as worse. That last whistle after we won't pin joy at getting out of the tunnel. It was pure wickedness of some sort. And what don't we'll soon know.'

'Likely enough,' said Frodo. 'But we could not have got even so far without him. So if we ever manage our errand, then Gollum and all his wickedness will be part of the plan.'

'So far you say,' said Sam. 'This far? Where are we now?'

'About at the crest of the main range of Ephel Dúath I guess,' said Frodo. 'Look! The road goes on now, it still went on up, but no longer steeply. Beyond and ahead there was an ominous glare in the sky, and like a great notch in the mountain wall a cleft was outlined against it.

On their right the wall of rock fell away and beyond ordered till it had no brink. Looking down Frodo saw into a vast darkness of the great ravine that was the head of Morghul dale. Deep in the depths as the faint glimmer of the ... it as... led on to the Morghul pass below. On their left sharp jagged pinnacles stood up like towers carved by the bitter years, and between them were very dark crevices and clefts. But to the left of the cleft there stood a red light. [K light] as a small black towers and between them there stood a red light.

'I don't like the look of that,' said Sam. 'This upper pass is guarded too. D'you remember the orcs would say if others or no. D'you think he's gone to fetch them — orcs or something?'

'No, I don't think so,' said Frodo. 'The Gap is no good, of course, but I don't think that he's gone to fetch orcs. Whatever it is, it's no slave of the Dark Lord.' 'I suppose not,' said Sam. 'No I suppose that the whole time it has been the way for poor Sméagol came. That's been his scheme. But how coming up here will help him, I can't guess.'

He was soon to learn.

Frodo went forward now — the last lap — and he exerted all his strength. He felt that if once he could get to the saddle of the pass and look over into the Nameless Land he would have accomplished something. Sam followed. He sensed evil all round him. He knew that they had walked into some trap, but what? He had sheathed his sword, but now he drew it in readiness. He halted for a moment, and stooped to pick up his staff with his left hand

Six books from six centuries

9-14

9 'The best state of a commonwealth'

Thomas More, *Libellus vere aureus nec minus salutaris quam festivus de optimo reip. statu, deq̨ nova insula Utopia*. [Louvain,] Theodoric Martin, [1516].

More's *Utopia* (which translates as 'Noplace'), 'no less instructive than entertaining', has been deemed by some a nostalgic recreation of the stabilities of medieval life, in contrast to the modern politics and economics of autocracy and agricultural enclosure; by others a foretaste of communism and the all-powerful state, with property held in common and a distinct lack of personal freedom. It opens with the sailor and explorer Raphael Hythlodaeus (that is 'expert in nonsense') condemning the practice of executing thieves and arguing that people will continue to steal so long as they face starvation. In Utopia all necessities are provided. Hythlodaeus lived on the island for five years, and describes the lives of its citizens to More and his friend Peter Gilles. In some ways the tale has a modern feel: Hythlodaeus interacts with real men other than his interlocutors—he voyaged with Amerigo Vespucci, he met Cardinal Morton on a

previous visit to England; a map of the island is supplied, along with its alphabet and examples of its language; it seeks to instruct by entertaining, and the wordplay of the names makes clear to those familiar with Greek that the story is a fantasy. *Utopia* was circulated to More's literary friends in order to elicit letters of praise (blurbs) which could be published with the text, and the whole idea is closely linked to the innovative thinking of Erasmus and his circle. It was immediately popular; the first edition was followed by one printed in Paris in 1517, two in Basle in 1518, and another in Florence in 1519. In the middle of the century there was a revival of interest: new editions in Latin were published and it was translated into German (1524), Italian (1548), French (1550), and, at last, English (1551). By the early seventeenth century 'Utopia' was used to mean 'a place, state, or condition ideally perfect in respect of politics, laws, customs, and conditions' (*OED*).

Purchased, 1952. *Arch. B e.44*

The complete works of St. Thomas More. Volume 4. Edited by E. Surtz and J.H. Hexter. New Haven and London, Yale University Press, 1965.

VTOPIAE INSVLAE FIGVRA

VTOPIENSIVM ALPHABETVM. 22.

a b c d e f g h i k l m n o p q r s t v x y
⊙⊖⊕⊙⊖⊙⊙⊂⊙∪⊖⊿⌐⌐⌐⌐⊓⌐⊓⊟⊞⊟⊟⊟⊟

Tetraſtichon vernacula Vtopienſium lingua.

Vtopos   ha   Boccas   peu   la

⊟⊞⊿⌐⊿⊟⊙⊙   ⊙⊿⊙⊙⊙⊟   ⌐⊙⊟⊟⊙

chama   polta   chamaan

⊙⊙⊿⊙ · ⌐⊿⊟⊞⊙   ⊙⊙⊿⊙⊙⌐

Bargol   he   maglomi   baccan

⊙⊙⊙⌐⊟   ⊂⊟   ⊿⊙⊙⊟⊿⊙   ⊙⊙⊙⊙⌐

ſoma   gymno   ſophaon

⊟⊿⊙   ⊃⊙⊿⌐   ⊟⌐⌐⊙⌐⌐

Agrama   gymnoſophon   labarembacha

⊙⌐⊙⊿⊙ · ⊃⊙⊿⌐⊟⌐⊙⌐⌐ · ⊙⊿⊙⊙⊙⊿⊙⊙⌐⊙

bodamiſomin

⊙⌐⊙⊙⊿⊙⊟⌐⊿⊙⌐

Voluala   barchin   heman   la

⊟⌐⊟⊟⊙⊙⊙ · ⊙⊙⊙⊙⊂⊙⌐ · ⊂⊙⊿⌐⊟⊙

lauoluola   dramme   pagloni.

⊙⊙⊟⌐⊟⌐⊟⊙ · ⊙⌐⊙⊿⊿⊙ · ⌐⊙⊙⊟⌐⊙

Horum verſuum ad verbum hæc eſt ſententia.

Vtopus me dux ex non inſula fecit inſulam
Vna ego terrarum omnium abſꝗ philoſophia
Ciuitatem philoſophicam expreſſi mortalibus
Libéter impartio mea, nó grauatim accipio meliora.

10 'curiously pasted together'

Michael Spaher, *An exact survey of the microcosmus or little world. Being an anatomie, of the bodies of man and woman … Usefull for all doctors, chirurgeons, &c. As also for painters, carvers … Englished by John Ireton.* London, printed by Joseph Moxon, 1670.

This first edition in English is based on Johann Remmelin's *Catoptrum microcosmicum* published by Spaher in Ulm in 1613. The three complex plates are pulls from the copperplates used in the 1667 edition published in Amsterdam, and retain their Dutch as well as Latin titles: Visio prima, De eerste plaet. Joseph Moxon, who had lived in Holland and spoke Dutch, is no doubt the source of the plates. A fourth, simple, plate, 'representing the skin with its vessels or veins under it', precedes the others.

In the Visio prima, representing a man and a woman, the male body has five layers above the skeleton, which is itself pasted to the mounting sheet, and some of these layers have extras attached. All the separate parts, and details therein, are keyed to the accompanying letterpress,

where they are given either their proper anatomical name or a brief description. The plates are described on the title-page thus: 'wherein the skin, veins, nerves, muscles, bones, sinews and ligaments, are accurately delineated. And curiously pasted together, so as at first sight you may behold all the outward parts of man and woman. And by turning up the several dissections of the paper take a view of all their inwards. With alphabetical referrences [*sic*] to every member and part of the body'. The second plate is of a man, the third of a woman.

In spite of the complexity of its production, the *Survey* was obviously found useful for other editions were published in 1675, 1691, 1695, 1702, and 1738. All editions are, not surprisingly, rare; the Bodleian has a copy of the 1695 printing, 'corrected by Clopton Havers', of which only two others are known. Of this first edition, only one other copy is recorded.

Acquired *c.*1810. *Arch. Nat. hist. P 9*

K.F. Russell, *British anatomy, 1525–1800. A bibliography of works published in Britain, America and on the Continent*. 2nd ed. Winchester, St. Paul's Bibliographies, 1987. No. 694.

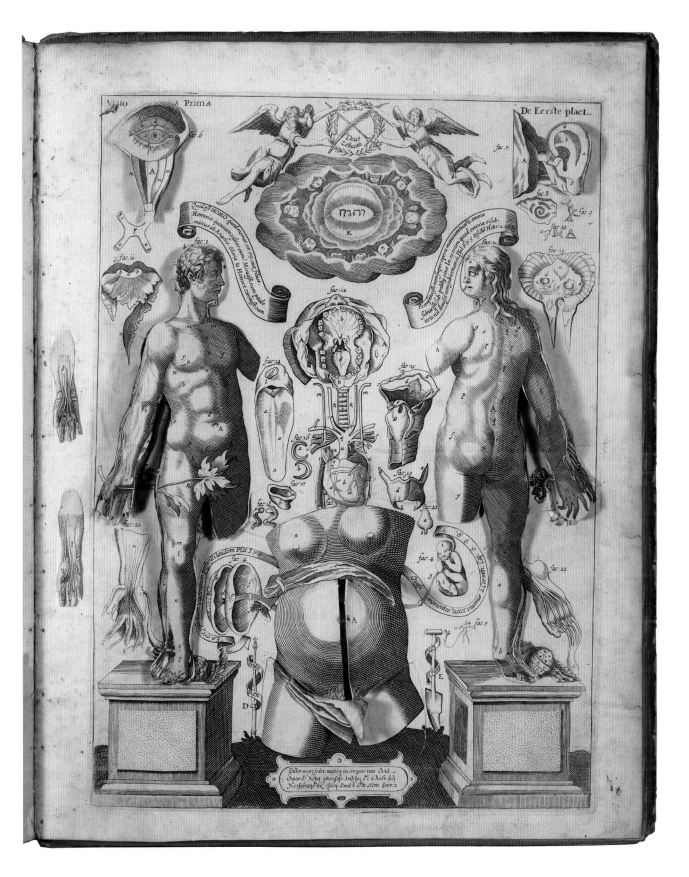

11 'The most important book to be published in England during the eighteenth century on the plants growing in a private garden'

Joannes Jacobus Dillenius, *Hortus Elthamensis, seu Plantarum rariorum quas in horto suo Elthami in Cantio coluit … Jacobus Sherard … delineationes et descriptiones …* Vol. 1. Londini, sumptibus auctoris, (typis G. Smith), 1732.

The German botanist Joannes Dillenius was invited to London in 1721 by William Sherard, one of the most distinguished botanists of his time, to assist him in arranging his collections and compiling a 'pinax or collection of all the names which had been given by botanical writers to each plant'. When he died in 1728 Sherard bequeathed his herbarium and botanical library to the University of Oxford and £3000 for the endowment of a professorship of botany, with the condition that Dillenius be appointed first Sherardian Professor. Sherard's brother James, an apothecary, had a garden at Eltham in Kent where he cultivated rare and exotic plants, and William had persuaded Dillenius to begin to draw and describe new plants in the garden in 1724. *Hortus Elthamensis* was published eight years later and won praise from fellow botanists for the accuracy of its drawings and descriptions. The book, printed on royal paper, contains 324 numbered plates with 417 drawings, plus one unnumbered at the end of the first volume. Dillenius engraved the plates himself and coloured some copies. One of these, finely bound in red morocco with coloured onlays and elaborate gold tooling, he bequeathed to the University with the instruction that it should be deposited in the Bodleian Library. Dillenius was not happy with the book, largely because it cost him so much money to have printed, and he blamed James Sherard for insisting it be so large and 'pompous'. In a letter to Sir John Kaye of 8 September 1737 he wrote: 'Besides ye Loss of Time & Labour, I loose by him [Sherard] at least 200 £. for it is a Book of but few Peoples' buying and therefore I do not think it safe to go through ye whole Impression. There were 500. Copies printed at his desire, (I would have printed but half so many) to which I got 145. copies of plates printed of[f], the rest I do not design to perfect.'

The Library has three other copies of this splendid book: one, with the plates not coloured, was presumably acquired soon after publication; two, one coloured and in a fine binding, the other uncoloured, were in the Radcliffe Library, which was transferred to the Bodleian by the Radcliffe Trustees over many years from the 1860s.

The specimens which Dillenius drew and described are now in the herbaria of the Department of Plant Sciences.

Bequeathed, 1747. *Arch. Nat. hist. H 10*

Blanche Henrey, *British botanical and horticultural literature before 1800.* London, Oxford University Press, 1975. No. 643.

Aster ericoides, Meliloti agrariæ umbone.

12 'The pleasing combination of Art and Nature adapted to the use of Man'

Humphry Repton, *Fragments on the theory and practice of landscape gardening. Including some remarks on Grecian and Gothic architecture, collected from various manuscripts …* London, printed by T. Bensley and Son, for J. Taylor, 1816.

Humphry Repton (1752–1818) came late to landscape gardening, but became the foremost practitioner of his time, assuming a position which had been more or less vacant since the death in 1783 of Lancelot 'Capability' Brown. Repton provided his patrons with watercolour drawings, often with 'slides' or overlays to give 'before' and 'after' views of the landscapes he would improve, accompanied by detailed reports on the work he proposed, often with asides on taste and aesthetics. These he had bound in red morocco to present to the landowners, and they became known as the Red Books. He also published his reflections on landscape gardening, basing them on the red books and having his drawings engraved and coloured for publication. *Fragments*, his last book, was 'selected from more than four hundred different Reports in MS.' and stands as a summation of his views; it includes the definition of landscape gardening quoted above.

Endsleigh was a farmhouse on the Duke of Bedford's Devon estate with fine views overlooking the Tamar; in 1809 the sixth duke decided to demolish it and build a hunting-lodge, or 'cottage'. Repton and his son submitted a plan for the new building, but a larger project by Jeffry Wyatville, on a site favoured by the duchess, was preferred. Wyatville was also commissioned to design the gardens, but when he failed to do very much, Repton was called in. He seemed reluctant at first (he was by now disabled as a result of an accident in 1811) but soon warmed to the prospect, seeing the opportunities the grounds offered for the picturesque: 'It is hardly necessary to remark how much the View from the House would be enlivened by the smoke of a Cottage on the opposite side of the water; and if this Cottage were to be a Mill, the occasional traffic and busy motion of persons crossing the Tamar, would add to the picturesque effect of a Landscape, which at present wants a little more animation.'

The mill wasn't built, but an empty cottage in the grounds had a fire lighted in it every day until 1946 for just this effect.

Acquired 1816? *Arch. AA c.13*

Stephen Daniels, *Humphry Repton, landscape gardening and the geography of Georgian England.* New Haven and London, Yale University Press for The Paul Mellon Centre for Studies in British Art, 1999.

13 'a vista of fairyland'

1908–09 Aurora Australis. Published at the winter quarters of the British Antarctic Expedition, 1907, during the winter months of April, May, June, July, 1908. Illustrated with lithographs and etchings; by George Marston. Printed at the sign of 'The Penguins'; by Joyce and Wild. Latitude 77° .. 32' South, longitude 166° .. 12' East, Antarctica.

With astonishing but characteristic boldness, Ernest Shackleton decided that to write, illustrate, print, and bind up to one hundred copies of a book would be a good way for the men on his expedition to pass the sunless Antarctic winter of 1908. To this end he persuaded the printing firm Sir Joseph Causton & Sons, Ltd. to give three weeks' training to the printers-to-be Ernest Joyce and Frank Wild, and the expedition's artist George Marston; in addition they gave him an Albion printing press, an etching press, types, ink (in three colours), and paper. In his Additional Preface Shackleton notes some of the constraints they overcame: 'owing to the low temperature in the hut, the only way to keep the printing ink in a fit state to use was to have a candle burning under the inking plate; and so, if some pages are printed more lightly than others it is due to the difficulty of regulating the heat, and consequently the thinning or thickening of the ink. Again the printing office was only six feet by seven and had to accommodate a large sewing machine and bunks for two men'. The contributions, in prose and verse, came from members

of the expedition, and mostly concern their life in the Antarctic; the reference to fairyland comes in an account of a dream: a walk by moonlight ('like some lovely transformation scene') and an encounter with a fantastic penguin. The printed sheets were bound by Bernard Day, using provision cases for the boards (this copy has '—D KIDNEYS' on the lower board); the sheepskin spine bears the title and the Penguin Press device stamped in blind. The book is signed by Shackleton and Marston. It is a really extraordinary piece of book production, and was described by Albert Ehrman as undoubtedly 'the most interesting of my modern imprints'.

The Broxbourne Library, named after the village they lived in, was formed by Ehrman and his wife between 1919 and 1969. It first concentrated on printing, particularly early printing, but also examples from 'out-of-the-way' places—hence *Aurora Australis*. Its scope was expanded to include fine and original bindings, early catalogues of printers, publishers, booksellers, auctioneers, and libraries, and type specimens. In 1971 the collection was deposited in the Bodleian, and in 1978 it was presented to the Library by John Ehrman, the collector's son (the type specimens were given to Cambridge University Library).

Presented through the Friends of the National Libraries, 1978. *Broxb. 51.14*

S.A. Spence, *Antarctic miscellany*. Ed. by J.J.H. & J.I. Simper. London, 1980. No. 1095.

14 'it is, at its best, the most powerful and compelling English version of Greek tragedy in existence'

**Aeschylus, Oresteia. A version by Ted Hughes,
woodcuts by Leonard Baskin. Choephori.** [Rockport:]
The Gehenna Press, 2001 [really 2002]. No. 11, of 60.

Ted Hughes's version of Aeschylus's trilogy had a post-humous premiere at the Cottesloe Theatre in late 1999;
the above quotation is from Michael Silk's review of a
performance in the *Times literary supplement*, 17 December 1999. Hughes, the most important English poet of
the second half of the 20th century, had a lasting and
keen interest in translating—his *Tales from Ovid*, 1997,
became a surprising best-seller. He had an equally last-ing and keen interest in the art of Leonard Baskin and
the work of his Gehenna Press. The two men became
friends in the 1950s and first collaborated on a broadside
edition of the poem 'Pike' in 1959. The Bodleian has two
of their more substantial productions: *Capriccio*, 1990,
and *Howls & whispers*, 1998. This edition of the *Oresteia*,
with its appropriately austere yet sumptuous appearance,
was published after the artist's death and is a stunning
memorial to both Baskin and Hughes. 'Sixty copies of
the *Oresteia* were printed at the Gehenna Press from early
Autumn of 2000 through the dry Spring of 2002. The
forty-seven woodcuts are printed from the cherry blocks

cut by Leonard Baskin. The paper is Zecchi, hand made
in Italy … The printing of the letterpress was achieved
by Arthur Larson & Daniel Keleher … Claudia Cohen
bound the edition.' This copy is being bought for the
Library by Bodley's American Friends and The Canadian
Friends of the Bodleian.

The Library has long had a strong interest in the
book arts, and fine printing and binding are well-represented in its collections. Since the revival of the
craft of printing by William Morris in the 19th century,
the Library has sought to acquire the publications of the
notable private presses. With the Broxbourne Collection
came an extraordinary amount of fine printing from the
early 20th century, and John Ryder supplied us with many
of the books published by the Officina Bodoni, and an
archive of correspondence with its proprietor Giovanni
Mardersteig, as well as many examples of private-press
work in general, both British and Continental. The
Library teaches printing using the Albion press once
worked by C.H.O. Daniel for printing books under the
Daniel Press imprint at Worcester College, where he was
Provost from 1903 till his death in 1919.

Presented, 2002. *Arch. C b.34/2*

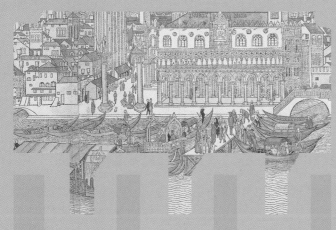

Medieval manuscripts

15–23

15 'The Oxford Roland'

Sir Kenelm Digby (1603–65) was still a young man when he gave nearly 240 manuscripts to the Bodleian in 1634, at the persuasion of Archbishop Laud. He had inherited the majority of them in 1632 from his Oxford tutor, Thomas Allen, whose greatest interest was in scientific and historical manuscripts. However, the most famous single book amongst them is the small, scruffy manuscript of *La Chanson de Roland*, the earliest surviving masterpiece of French literature. This Anglo-Norman copy crystallizes the epic poem at a stage perhaps around the second quarter of the 12th century. It may well have been in the Oxford area since the 13th century, for it is bound with another book which had been bequeathed by 1263 to Osney Abbey.

Presented, 1634. *MS. Digby 23, fol. 32r*

S ire Rollt y uoffire oliuer·

p ur deu uos pri ne uos cuntraliez·

j a li corners ne nos aureit mester·

oi ais ne pur quant si eft il aser melz·

y engez li reis si nus purrat uenger·

j a cil despaigne ne sen dement cher liez·

N tre franceis i descendrut a pied·

t ruuere nos y mozy de trenchiez·

l euerunt nos en bieres sur sumers·

S i nus plurrunt de doel y de pieie·

e nfuerunt en aitres demusters·

N en mangerunt ne lu ne porc ne chen·

R espunt Rollt sire mult dites bien. AOI.

R oll ad mis lolifan a sa buche·

empeint le ben par grant uertut le sunet·

h alt sunt li pui y la uoiz est mult lunge·

G rant· xxx· liwes loirent il respundre·

k arles loit y sescumpaignes tutes·

c o dit li reis bataille funt nre hume·

e guenelun li respundit encuntre·

S altre le desist ia semblast grant mencunge· AOI

l i quens Rollt par peine y par ahans·

p ar grant dulor sunet sun olifan·

p ar mi la buche en salt fors li cler sancs·

D e sun ceruel le tiple en est rupant·

D el corn qui l tient loie en est mult grant·

k arles lentent ki est as porz passant·

N aimes li duc loid sil escultent li fran·

16 'The Junius Psalter'

Few if any of the great donors of manuscripts to the Bodleian can have used the Library as intensively themselves as did Francis Junius. Born in Heidelberg to a French Protestant refugee family, Junius spent many years in England, where in 1621 he became librarian to the collector and patron Thomas Howard, Earl of Arundel. For his work on the languages of northern Europe, which included the production of a Gothic glossary, Junius is recognized as one of the founders of the discipline of comparative philology. He was also the paramount influence in the building up of Anglo-Saxon studies in Oxford, where he came to live towards the end of his life to be near his old pupil Thomas Marshall, the Rector of Lincoln College. Junius's gift just before his death included the medieval manuscripts and early printed books in his possession, his scholarly papers and transcripts (some of which now provide a unique record

of lost or damaged originals), and the printing types (including Anglo-Saxon and Gothic) which he had had struck for his own publications.

The attraction of this manuscript for Junius probably consisted less in the inventive and varied ornamental initials with which each Psalm begins, important though these are for their blend of insular and continental elements, than in the continuous interlinear gloss which provides an Old English translation above the Latin words. The manuscript was produced in the first half of the 10th century, perhaps at Winchester; its calendar notes the obits of King Alfred and his queen Ealswith. It is also known as the 'Codex Vossianus', since Junius acquired it from his nephew Isaac Vossius, who was librarian to Queen Christina of Sweden.

Presented, 1677. *MS. Junius 27, fol. 27v*

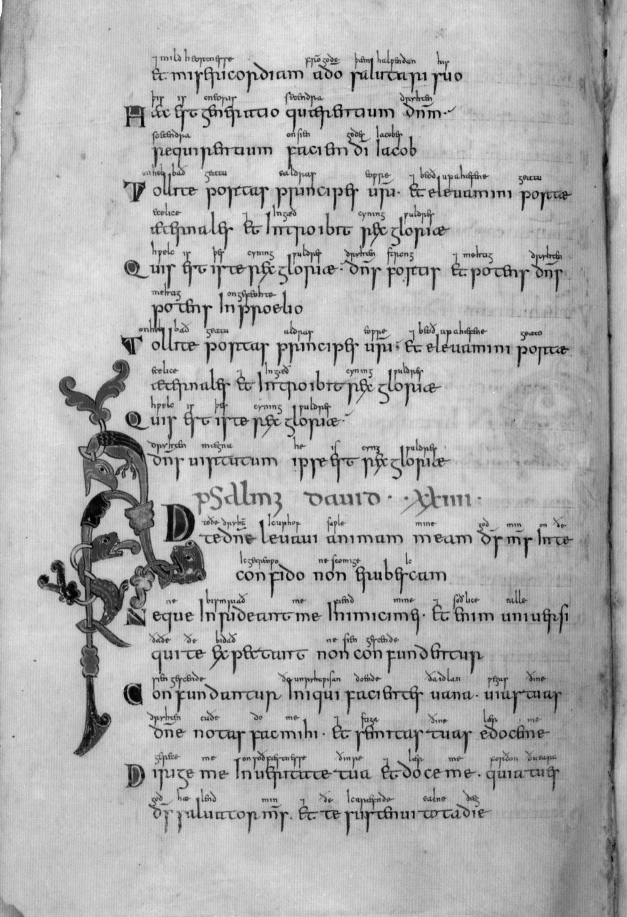

et misericordiam a deo salutari suo

Hec est generatio quirentium dominum

requirentium faciem di Iacob

Tollite portas principes uras et eleuamini porta

eternales et introibit rex glorie

Quis est iste rex glorie dominus fortis et potens dominus

potens in proelio

Tollite portas principes uras et eleuamini porta

eternales et introibit rex glorie

Quis est iste rex glorie

dominus uirtutum ipse est rex glorie

Psalmz dauid · XXIIII ·

Ad te domine leuaui animam meam deus meus in te

confido non erubescam

Neque inrideant me inimici mei · et enim uniuersi

qui te expectant non confundentur

Confundantur iniqui facientes uana · uniuersi

domine notas fac mihi · et semitas tuas edoce me

Dirige me in ueritate tua et doce me · quia tu

deus saluator meus · et te sustinui tota die

17 'The Annals of Inisfallen'

'Where your treasure is, there will your heart be also.'
Richard Rawlinson (1690–1755) bequeathed his heart to St.
John's College and his collections to Oxford University.
The Rawlinson bequest, the Bodleian's largest accession
of the 18th century, included a major group of Irish
manuscripts which he had bought at auction in 1747. These
had had various English owners after being collected by
Sir James Ware (1594–1666), Auditor-General of Ireland.
The oldest surviving manuscript of any Irish historical

text is this year-by-year chronicle in Irish and Latin, first
compiled in Munster around 1092. Later, at the island
monastery of Inisfallen in the lower Lake of Killarney, it
was continuously updated by some 38 successive hands up
to the 14th century, with yet more later additions. On the
left-hand page, a 15th-century hand adds a record for 1450
to the earlier annals for 1271–76.

Bequeathed, 1756. *MS. Rawl. B. 503, fol. 48v*

Cobair nig fraine ⁊ noам aiñe dee
dedul iſ tir nairi.

1272

At enкaiñ fⱸgⱸaḋ ⁊ xxuiii fuini
doneⱡ moꝛ tꝛi bliaⱸai ꝼ ⁊ eⱸgⱸⱸ
coitⱸ ceñ et gⱡlⱡib ⁊ gⱸedelⱡib inⱨ
nen ⁊ goꝛta moꝛ tꝛi bliaⱸai ceⱸⱨ
coꝛ iⱡⱡb roⱸanⱸi doiⱡɫet ⁊ doogx
tⱡ ⱸⱨiⱸ. dodⱸmib boⱸta ⁊ gⱨꝛeñ
uⱸⱸ doⱸⱨib ꝛⱸⱸobꝛi. gluogeⱶ lagⱡⱡ
lyⱸⱸeñ m neſiuni gudm nⱡliꝛe . imⱶⱶ aⱡ
ſen gan oleⱸodeⱸⱸⱨ mnuⱡⱸno . na gⱡll ⱸⱨⱸa ⱶ
dul go loñneⱸ aⱡ y bꝛiⱸ ⁊ ſiⱸ doⱸⱸⱸb ꝛⱼ aⱸ

bᵃ

ⱸ do gⱸuⱸⱸ oⱸ.uⱡⱡe de buꝛe ⱸⱸ ꝛeⱸ
nⱸⱸa . ⁊ ſⱸⱸⱶ do tⱸbⱸ guⱸⱸ ſⱡⱡeⱡ

mᶜ clxxiiii Henaiꝛ foꝛ iny ⁊ xx ꝼꝛi ⁊ bliaⱸm biꝛ ſeñ aⱸ
xix i deⱸmⱸⱸⱸⱸⱡ ⱸido . Riⱸⱸⱸ de kⱸꝛⱸⱸ degⱸ
⁊ geⱸⱸ igⱸ baⱸⱸ moⱸ hmoⱸⱸⱡ . ſeneſⱸⱡ deⱸⱸⱸ .

At euui . fⱸmⱸ xꝛi ꝛuⱼꝛe . eⱸgⱸⱸ
aⱡ do nⱡⱡⱡ oⱸⱸ y̆ⱸⱸⱡyⱸ do иⱸ buⱸ
ⱡⱸ euⱸ do ⱸⱡⱸⱸ toⱼⱸⱸ . ⱡ le ⱸⱸⱶⱸⱸ
ⱸⱸb ⱸⱸ ꝛ ꝼeⱸⱸⱸ gⱸⱸ ⱸⱸⱸ ꝛ ꝼⱡⱸ
nⱸⱡy ⱸⱸⱸ yꝛeⱸⱸⱨib ⱸⱸ ⱷⱸⱸ ꝼ ⱡⱸ ⱸ
noⱡⱡⱸⱸ ⱸⱸⱸⱡⱸ ⱸⱸⱸⱸⱡ y do иⱸⱸ
ⱸⱸ ꝛoꝛ ⱸⱸ ⱸⱸⱸⱸⱸ ⱸ ⱸⱸ ꝼⱸⱸⱸⱸ
иⱸ ⱸⱸⱡⱸⱸⱸ иⱸ ⱸonⱡⱡ oⱸⱸ y̆ⱸⱸⱡⱸ
ⱡ tⱸⱸⱸ . ⁊ uⱸⱸ ⱡⱸⱼ ꝼuⱸⱸ ⱸⱼⱸⱸⱸ
oⱸ ⱸⱸ ⱡⱡo ⱸⱸ . ⱸⱸ ⱸ ⱸⱸⱸ ⱸyⱼ
ⱸⱸ guⱼⱸuⱸⱼⱸⱼmo

1450

ⱡ ꝛⱼ ꝼ bⱡⱸⱸⱸm do ⱸ ⱸ ⱸ ꝛuⱸⱸ
oꝼuⱡⱡ ⱸⱸ ꝼonⱸⱸⱸⱸ ⱸⱸⱸ a eⱸ y
ⱸⱼⱸ ꝼⱸⱸⱸⱸ ⱸⱸ ⱸⱸⱸ ⱸⱸ
иⱸⱸⱸ oⱸ ⱸꝼⱸⱸⱸ deⱸ ⱡeⱸⱸ . ⱸⱸⱸⱸ
ⱸⱸ ⱸⱸⱸ иⱸ ꝛ иⱸ ⱸ

Henaiꝛ ꝼ domñaⱨ . ⁊ xx .
ſuꝛꝛⱸ ⱸ ⱸ ⱸ ⱸ

At euⱸⱸⱸ ꝼ aⱸⱸⱸ xꝛi ꝛuⱼⱼe . ⱡⱡ
ⱸⱸ ⱸⱨⱸ ⱸⱸⱸ ꝼⱸⱸ ⱸyⱸⱸⱸⱸ guⱸ
aꝛ ⱸ ⱸⱨⱼⱸⱸⱸ y aꝛ ⱸeⱼⱸe иꝛ gⱸⱡⱡ
aꝛy иⱼ ꝼꝛⱸⱸⱸⱸⱸ ⱸyⱸⱸⱸⱨ
ⱸⱸⱸⱨⱸⱸ ⱼⱸⱸⱨ y̆ⱸ meⱸ . ⱡ ⱸⱼⱼ
иⱸⱶ m ceⱸⱸⱨⱸ ꝛⱸⱸⱨⱼⱸⱨ ⱸⱸ ⱸⱨⱸ
иⱸⱸ deⱸⱸⱼy y иⱸⱼⱸⱨ oⱸo ⱸⱸⱼⱸ
auⱨⱸⱸ . ⱶ ⱡⱨⱡⱸ ⱸⱸⱨⱨ iиⱨⱨ . ⱡ
ⱶ ꝼⱸⱸⱨⱸ иⱨ goꝛⱼoꝛⱸ uꝛⱡⱸ ⱶ
иⱨⱨⱨⱸ y̆ do иⱨⱡⱸⱸⱸ . ⱡ ⱸⱨⱡⱸ ⱸⱶ
y bⱸⱨⱨ uꝛ le иⱸⱨⱨⱨ иⱨ aⱨ
ⱸⱨ иⱨⱨⱸ ceиⱸⱨꝛⱨ y̆ le ⱸⱨиⱸ ⱸⱨ
ⱶ eⱨⱨⱨⱨⱸ ꝼ ⱨⱨⱨⱨ . y uⱨⱨⱨⱨ

Henaiꝛ ꝼ luan . ⁊ xxx ꝼꝛ

ⱸⱨⱸ иⱸ ⱸⱨⱨⱡⱸ do иⱨⱸⱨ ꝼeⱨⱨ
иⱸ ⱸ uⱨ иⱨ . ⱡ . do toⱼⱸⱨ aⱨ ꝼⱸⱨⱨ
ⱶⱨⱨⱡⱸ aꝛ иⱸ eⱨⱨⱨ ꝛ ꝼ do ⱷⱨⱸⱸ
do иⱨⱨⱨ aⱨ aⱼ иⱸⱸ ⱸoⱨⱨⱨⱨ

Henaiꝛ ꝼ maꝛⱸ . xꝛi ꝼꝛi
ⱸ eⱸ iⱨ ꝼⱨⱨⱸ

ꝛⱨm i . иⱸⱨⱨꝼ ⱸⱡⱡe y̆ ⱸⱨⱨe ⱼⱨe
meⱸ diꝼⱨ иⱨ ꝼⱸⱨⱸⱨⱸbⱡⱸⱼⱼ y̆ꝛ ꝼ

18   Polyphonic music in a Canonici manuscript

In 1817, Oxford University bought over 2000 medieval manuscripts from the heirs of Matteo Luigi Canonici of Venice (1727–1805/6), more than half his collection. At the time, the purchase would have been justified by the wealth of manuscripts of the Greek and Latin classics, but the finest treasures took some time to be recognized. This manuscript emerged, on its publication by Sir John Stainer in 1895, as Oxford's most important source for medieval music. It was copied in Italy perhaps around 1428 to 1436, and contains 326 pieces of which 216 are not known elsewhere. Its publication more than doubled the known repertory of Dufay and Binchois, revealed the names of some eighteen new composers, and demonstrated an almost forgotten genre of secular songs in French and Italian. The left-hand page, with Dufay's name at the top, shows his song for three voices, 'Ce moys de May'.

Purchased, 1817.   *MS. Canon. Misc. 213, fol. 17v*

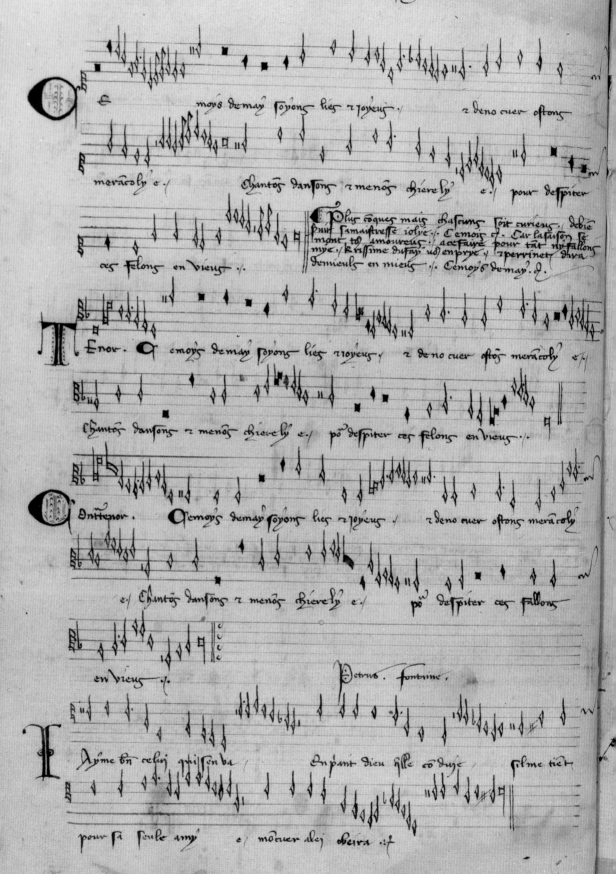

19 'The Douce ivory'

Francis Douce left most of his antiquities (objects other than books, manuscripts, coins and prints) to his friend the antiquary (and authority on arms and armour) Sir Samuel Rush Meyrick, whose catalogue of his 'Doucean Museum' published in 1836 contains descriptions of over fifty ivories. However, at least two ivories did come as part of Douce's bequest to the Bodleian because they were attached to medieval manuscripts. Before the French Revolution this one had belonged to the abbey of St. Faron at Meaux. It was bought at M. Abel Remusat's sale in Paris in 1833 by Messrs. Payne, the London booksellers, and acquired from them by Douce later the same year for £31 10s.

The manuscript inside is a Gospel lectionary for Benedictine use, written (in the recently reformed script now known as Caroline minuscule) and decorated by nuns at the convent of Chelles near Paris (where Charlemagne's sister Gisla was abbess) in about the year 800. The ivory panel of approximately the same date which is set into the manuscript's upper cover represents at its centre the triumphant Christ trampling on a lion and a serpent (cf. Psalm 90 (91), verse 13). The organization of the panel, as well as the details of the smaller scenes from the life of Christ which surround the central figure, are typical of the ivories produced in Charlemagne's court school at Aachen in being modelled on Late Antique ivory diptychs: six of the scenes are evidently copied from two surviving fragments from the early 5th century, now preserved in Paris and Berlin. The subject-matter of the ivory is clearly appropriate for a book containing Gospel readings for the Mass through the year, but it is not clear at what stage ivory and manuscript were joined together: the remainder of the present binding is 18th-century.

Bequeathed, 1834. *MS. Douce 176, upper cover*

20 'The Ashmole Bestiary'

Elias Ashmole's collecting and research activities ranged widely in the fields of astronomy, astrology, alchemy, botany, genealogy, heraldry, numismatics, and magic. The Ashmole Bestiary is one of several items in his collection of manuscripts and printed books to have previously belonged to John Tradescant the elder: it was almost certainly seen by a German student, Georg Christoph Stirn, when he visited Tradescant's museum in Lambeth in 1638. Tradescant's collection of human and natural 'curiosities' had become one of the sights of London: it was known as the 'Ark' (just as Francis Bacon had described Bodley's new library as 'an ark to save learning from deluge'), and was further enhanced by John Tradescant the younger, a traveller, botanist, and royal gardener like his father. Ashmole paid for the publication of, and partly wrote, the catalogue of the Tradescant collection which appeared in 1656; but the catalogue did not include descriptions of any of the books or manuscripts in the collection. Having acquired the Tradescants' rarities from John the younger, Ashmole presented them to Oxford University, where they were housed in the specially constructed Ashmolean Museum. There the Tradescants' books must have been mixed up with Ashmole's own, which he bequeathed in 1692; the whole library was transferred to the Bodleian from the Ashmolean only in the nineteenth century.

The medieval Latin Bestiary, like the Late Antique *Physiologus* on which it was based, is a Christianized version of ancient natural history. It describes the natures and habits assigned to the members of the animal kingdom by the Creator so that human beings may learn the way to redemption from their example. Sailors who beach their boat and light their fires on the back of a whale, for instance, believing it to be an island, will be dragged down into the water when the whale feels the heat and dives into the depths; in the same way, those who in their ignorance put their trust in the devil will be plunged into the fires of Gehenna with him. The picture cycles in several of the manuscripts are closely related to each other, though they are almost entirely medieval, not Late Antique, in origin; they illustrate the creatures and associated stories, but not the moralizations. A mere handful of the animals described were native to Europe, the remainder being known only from written reports and traditional illustrations. Produced at an unknown location in England in *c.*1200–1210, the Ashmole manuscript is one of the finest of the early Gothic illuminated Bestiaries which were especially popular in England in the first half of the 13th century.

Bequeathed to the University, 1692, transferred to the Bodleian, 1860. *MS. Ashmole 1511, fol. 86v*

officium habeant. Amphi enim grece. utrumq; dr. i. op inaquis ͛ interis uiuunt. ut foce. cocodrilli ypota mu. h. est equi fluctuales. ☩ DE BALENA.

St belua inmari q̃ grece aspido delone dr. latine ũ aspido testudo. lete ꝫ dicta. ob immanitatem cor poris. ē enim sic ille qui excepit ionam. cuius aluus tante magnitudinis fuit ut putaret̃ infernus dicen

21 Byzantine Gospels from Holkham Hall

The Bodleian's most important 20th-century accession of Greek manuscripts came from Holkham Hall in Norfolk. Holkham had been built by Thomas Coke, Earl of Leicester (1697–1759), to house the treasures which he had collected during his Grand Tour. He bought this fine early 13th-century Gospels in 1718, at the Berlin sale of the collector A.E. Seidel who had first brought it to the west. The portrait of St. Luke is displayed, at the start of his Gospel. The Bodleian purchased the main group of 112 Greek manuscripts from the 5th Earl of Leicester in 1954, with generous help from the Dulverton Trust.

A further 47 manuscripts in other languages were bought with the aid of the Pilgrim Trust in 1956. Holkham's remaining three Greek manuscripts, including this one, came in 1981: they were assigned by the government to the Bodleian, with a few other fine illuminated manuscripts, in part satisfaction of Capital Transfer Tax after the death of the 5th Earl. Other medieval manuscripts from Holkham are now at the British Library and elsewhere, but many still remain at the Hall.

Presented, 1981. *MS. Holkham Gr. 114, fol. 88v*

22 'The St. George's Hours'

Through the generosity of the Friends of the Bodleian, the Library was recently able to acquire this fragmentary later 14th-century Book of Hours, which had previously been in the collection of the bookseller William Foyle. Though its use is the widespread one of Sarum, the manuscript's specifically Oxford connection is revealed in its calendar, where the original red-letter entry for 2 April reads 'Dedicacio sancti georgii oxonie'. St. George's Oxford was the church founded within Oxford castle; control of it had passed in the 12th century to the Augustinian abbey of Osney. The manuscript must have been made either for one of the ministers or Augustinian canons who served the church, or for a student or lay-person connected with it. A number of later inscriptions in the calendar all relate to families in the Shropshire area.

The three surviving historiated initials are enough to reveal that the iconographic programme for the Hours of the Virgin consisted of a cycle of scenes from the Passion of Christ. This is a common feature in English Books of Hours, but differs from the French pattern of scenes from the Life of the Virgin. It is very likely that the manuscript was written and illuminated within Oxford itself. Though illumination from 13th-century Oxford, the age of William de Brailes, is now familiar to art historians, thanks partly to the work done on Oxford property records, relatively little is known about Oxford illumination in the following century. The manuscript will therefore provide important evidence for the development of book production and illumination in Oxford at this period. Surprisingly, there appears to be no other Book of Hours with an established origin in Oxford currently in the possession of any Oxford library.

About the end of the 15th century, St. George's was reorganized by Osney abbey as a small college, the manuscript statutes of which arrived in the Bodleian as part of the Rawlinson bequest (MS. Rawl. statutes 34).

Purchased, 2000. *MS. Don. d. 206, fol. 30v*

Speciosa facta es et suauis. In deliciis tuis
sancta dei genitrix. Dne exaudi oratione meam.
Et clamor: oro. Concede nos famulos.

Ora sexta ihc est cruci conclaua
tus et est cum latronibus pen
dens deputatis pre tormentis siciens
felle saturatus. agnus tamen diluit
sic luctificatus. Adoramus te ✝. Qui
p scdam crucem. oro. Domine ihu ✝.

Ad nonam.
Deus in adiu
torium meu
intende. o
mine ad ad
iuuandum
me festina.
lia pri sicut erat. Alla. Me
mento. Maria lia tibi dne
qui natus es. ✝. Germinauit radix.

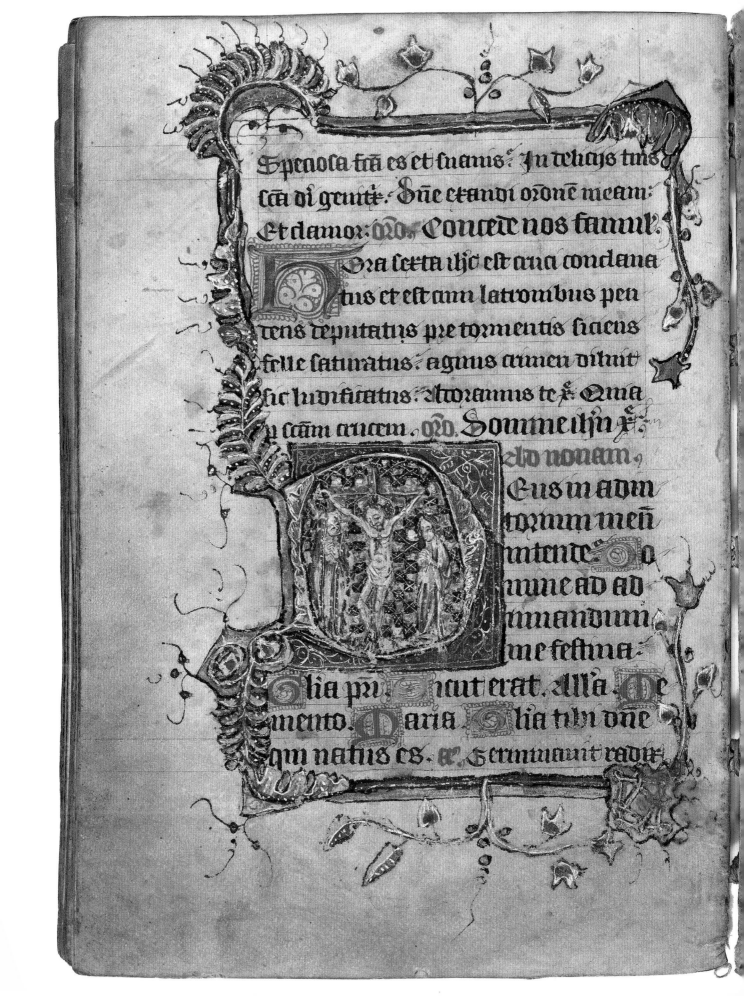

23 'The Laudian Acts'

William Laud was Sir Thomas Bodley's natural successor as a fount of donations and as an inspiration to other donors. By encouraging the 3rd Earl of Pembroke to buy the Barocci manuscripts for Oxford in 1629, he founded the Bodleian's pre-eminent collection of Greek manuscripts. As Chancellor of the University, Archbishop Laud sought out books in many languages and presented them in successive donations from 1633 to 1641. He obtained many early manuscripts from Germany, including this copy of the Acts of the Apostles in Greek and Latin from St.

Kylian's Cathedral, Würzburg. Its gift in 1636 seems to have marked its return to England, for in the early 8th century its bilingual text had been used in Northumbria by Bede himself, most likely from this very manuscript. It had been written around 600, perhaps in Sardinia. It is the earliest surviving manuscript fully to incorporate Acts chapter 8 verse 37, where the Ethiopian eunuch declares his belief in Jesus as the Son of God.

Presented, 1636. *MS. Laud Gr. 35, fol. 70v*

eunuchus	ο ευνουχος
ecce	ϊδου
aqua	υδωρ
quid	τι
prohibetme	κωλυειμε
baptizari	βαπτισθηναι
dixitautem	ειπενδε
ei	αυτω
philippus	οφιλιππος
sicredis	εανπιστευεις
extoto	εξολης
corde	τηςκαρδιαςσου
salvusfiseris	σωθησει
respondensautem	αποκριθεισδε
dixit	ειπεν
credo	πιστευω
inchristum	εις τονχν
filium	τονυιον
dei	τουθυ
etiussit	καιεκελευσεν
stare	στηναι
currum	τοαρμα
etdescenderunt	καικατεβησαν
inaquam	εις τουδωρ
uterque	αμφοτεροι
philippusquoque	οτεφιλιππος

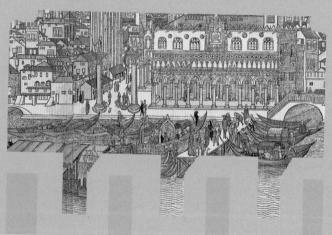

Books printed before 1501

24–30

24 *Biblia Latina* [Mainz: Johann Gutenberg & Johann Fust, *c.*1455].

'The Gutenberg Bible' is probably one of the most well-known of all books printed. Johann Gensfleisch zum Gutenberg (*c.*1397–1468), a goldsmith from Mainz, is the man who has traditionally been credited with the invention of printing in the West with moveable type. Perhaps his most singular achievement was really the invention of a method for manufacturing such type. How he actually did this has exercised the minds of bibliographers and printers for generations: now, in the digital age, this question is being examined again, this time with the aid of computer technology. Each piece of type was supposedly cast from a mould so that each individual letter 'a', for example, would be the same: however, the use of superimposed digitized images has shown the great variety of forms for the same letter, which appear on any one page of this and other productions of Gutenberg's; scholars from Princeton are currently trying to find explanations for this. To Gutenberg must also be assigned the credit for the preparation of an ink which would adhere to metal types, and, presumably, for at least the start of the process by which the wine press was transformed into the printing press.

What is clear, however, is that Gutenberg had been working on printing with moveable type for many years, indeed, probably from the time he was in exile in Strasbourg in the early 1440s. He seems to have experimented with smaller productions, and, on his return to Mainz in the late 1440s, to have entered a partnership with a lawyer, Johann Fust, who provided the financial support for the project (at least 1600 guilders). The product of this collaboration was the 'Gutenberg' or '42-line Bible', the work shown here. That the first substantial book to be printed in Europe was a Bible is clearly no coincidence. Although the Bible in the Vulgate Latin translation did not constitute a completely uniform body of texts, the Latin Bible was an 'international' text, used throughout Europe, and so an ideal choice as a book for which sales would be guaranteed. The Gutenberg Bible comes from the textual tradition of the Parisian Bibles: this had most international currency in Europe north of the Alps from the 13th century. Later other northern European editions were printed from the Gutenberg Bible, reinforcing, at least for a time, the prevalence of this version.

It was probably Fust's business acumen which ensured that all copies of the Bible were sold before printing was finished. This is known from Enea Silvio Piccolomini, later Pope Pius II, who was Papal Legate

Incipit ꝓlogus beati ieronimi
presbiteri in libros machabeorum.

Machabeoꝛu libri duo ꝓno-
tant prelia inter hebreoꝛ
duces gentiumq̃ persaꝛu:
pugnã q̃ sabbatoꝛ ⁊ no-
biles machabei ducis triũphos: ex cui⁹
noie ⁊ libri ⁊de̅ su̅t nu̅cupati. Hec q̃
historia cõtinet etiã inclita illa gesta
machabeoꝛ fratrũ: qui sub antiochp
rege pro sacris legibꝫ dira toꝛmenta
perpessi sunt. Quos mater pia dum
diuersis supplicijs urgeret̃ non solũ
nõ fleuit: sed et gaudes hoꝛtabat̃ ad
gloriã passionis. Explicit ꝓlogus
Incipit liber primus machabeorum.

Et factũ est postq̃ꝫ per-
cussit alexander phi-
lippi rex macedo qui
primus regnauit i
grecia egressus de ter-
ra cethim dariũ regẽ
persaꝛu ⁊ medoꝛ. o̅stituit prelia multa:
et obtinuit omniũ municiones: et in-
terfecit reges terre. Et ꝑtrãsijt usqꝫ ad
fines terre: ⁊ accepit spolia m̅ltitudinis
gentiũ: ⁊ siluit terra in o̅spectu eius. Et
cõgregauit uirtutẽ ⁊ exercitũ foꝛtem ni-
mis: et exaltatũ est et eleuatũ coꝛ ei⁹: et
obtinuit regiones gentiũ ⁊ tirannos
et facti sunt illi in tribut̅. Et post hec
decidit in lectũ: ⁊ cognouit quia moꝛe-
ret̃. Et uocauit pueꝛos suos nobiles
qui secũ erant nutriti a iuuentute sua:
et diuisit illis regnũ suũ cum adhuc
uiueret. Et regnauit alexander annis
duodecim: ⁊ moꝛtu⁹ ẽ. Et obtinuerũt
pueri ei⁹ regnũ unusquisqꝫ i loco suo:
et impoꝛuerũt omnes sibi diademata
post moꝛte ei⁹ ⁊ filij eoꝛ post eos annis
m̅ltis: et m̅ltiplicata su̅t mala i terra.
Et exijt ex eis radix pꝛcati antiochus

illustris fili⁹ antiochi regis qui fuerat
rome obses: et regnauit in anno cen-
tesimotricesimo et septimo regni greco-
rum. In diebꝫ illis exierunt ex isrl filij
iniqui: ⁊ suaserũt m̅ltas dicentes. Ea-
mus ⁊ disponam⁹ testamentũ cũ gen-
tibus que circa nos su̅t: quia exquo
recessim⁹ ab eis inuenerũt nos multa
mala. Et bonus uisus ẽ sermo i oclꝫ
eoꝛ. Et destinauerũt aliqui de ꝓ̅lo ⁊
abierũt ad regẽ: et dedit illis poꝛestatẽ
ut faceret iusticiã gentiũ. Et edificaue-
rũt gymnasiũ in iherosolimis scdm
leges nacõnũ: ⁊ fecerũt sibi ꝓputia: ⁊ re-
cesserũt a testamento sancto: ⁊ iuncti su̅t
nationibꝫ: et uenũdati sunt ut faceret̅
malũ. Et paratũ ẽ regnũ in conspectu
antiochi: ⁊ cepit regnare i terra egipti:
ut regnaret sup duo regna. Et intrauit
in egiptũ in m̅ltitudine graui in curri-
bus ⁊ elephantis ⁊ equitibꝫ: ⁊ copiosa
nauiũ m̅ltitudine. Et constituit bellũ
aduersus ptolomeũ regẽ egipti: ⁊ ueri-
tus ẽ ptolomeus a facie eius ⁊ fugit:
et recideru̅t uulnerati m̅lti. Et compre-
hendit ciuitates munitas in terra egipti: ⁊ accepit spolia terre egipti. Et con-
uertit antiochus postq̃ꝫ pcussit egiptũ
in centesimo ⁊ q̃dragesimo ⁊ tercio anno ⁊ ascendit ad isrl: et ascendit iherosolimis i m̅ltitudine graui. Et intrauit
in sanctificatione cũ supbia: ⁊ accepit
altare aureũ ⁊ candelabrũ luminis ⁊
uniuersa uasa eius ⁊ mensam ꝓposi-
cionis ⁊ libatoria ⁊ fialas ⁊ moꝛario-
la aurea ⁊ uelũ ⁊ coronas ⁊ oꝛnamen-
tum aureum qd in facie templi erat: ⁊
cõminuit oĩa. Et accepit argentum ⁊
aurũ et uasa co̅cupiscibilia: et accepit
thesauros occultos quos inuenit: et
sublatis omnibꝫ abijt i terrã suã. Et
fecit cedem hominũ: et locutus est in

17

at the Imperial Diet in Frankfurt am Main in October 1454, and, whilst there, saw several gatherings of the book displayed, probably before production was finished. He explained that between approximately 160 and 180 copies were being made. But he was unable to obtain a copy for Cardinal Juan de Carvajal, for all had been sold in advance. Samples had also been sent to the Emperor. Unfortunately, the business-partnership between Gutenberg and Fust collapsed at some point after the printing of the Bible, when Fust foreclosed on Gutenberg. It was at this time that the bulk of Gutenberg's presses and types went to Peter Schoeffer, who was subsequently to marry Fust's daughter. Gutenberg, however, was able to continue to print until about 1460, and lived on in Mainz until 1468.

The first owner of the Bodleian's copy (open here to show the fine contemporary manuscript initials and finishing in blue and red) was probably Erhard Neninger (c.1420–1475), who was Mayor of Heilbronn: he presented the book to the Carmelite house in Heilbronn not later than 1474. This is known because an inscription on the original binding (which has since been lost in the rebinding, for which see below) was recorded by François-Xavier Laire in his *Index librorum*

ab inventa typographia ad annum 1500. The Bible was clearly in the possession of the city of Heilbronn by the early seventeenth century, for it was presented by the city to the great Swedish statesman, Axel Oxenstierna (1583–1654) in 1633, the year in which the latter brought the Protestant princes of Germany into the (short-lived) League of Heilbronn. The provenance is then unknown until it appears in the library of the French ecclesiastic and political figure, Cardinal Étienne Charles de Loménie de Brienne (1727–1794). The Cardinal had the Bible rebound in middle/late 1780s by the well-known French binder Nicolas-Denis Derome le jeune (1731–c.1788), who gave the two volumes their present elegant gold-tooled green morocco bindings. The Bodleian purchased this copy in 1793 for what was then the relatively small sum of £100.

Purchased, 1793. *Arch. B b.11, fol. 162r and binding*

A Continental shelf: books across Europe from Ptolemy to Don Quixote. An exhibition to mark the re-opening of the Bodleian Exhibition Room (Oxford: Bodleian Library, 1994), no. 16.
S.H. Steinberg, *Five hundred years of printing*. New ed., revised by John Trevitt (London: British Library, 1996).

25 Gaius Plinius Secundus, *Historia naturalis*, trans. Cristoforo Landino. Venice: Nicolaus Jenson, 1476.

This spectacular edition of Pliny represents a combination of Florentine entrepreneurial skills with Venetian technical expertise. It was printed by Jenson in Venice for the Strozzi family, the Florentine merchants and bankers. Filippo Strozzi (1428–1491) and his brother, Lorenzo, financed this edition. They paid Cristoforo Landino (1424–1492) 50 gold florins for the translation into Italian: Landino had already produced a translation of the *Natural history* for King Ferdinand I of Naples (1458–94), and then offered this translation to the Strozzi brothers, whilst, at the same time, accepting their payment for his work! When printing was finished Jenson handed over all 1023 copies (1000 on paper, the rest on parchment) to the Strozzi, who checked the books, and informed Jenson that four were wanting two sheets. Copies were subsequently sold in several Italian cities, and sent to Bruges and London: the paper copies were to retail at seven florins each.

This copy is printed on parchment, and was specially bound and hand-illuminated for Filippo Strozzi himself by the Florentine illuminator Monte di Giovanni di Miniato (1448–1529). The bills for the work survive and it took four years for the job to be completed, at a cost (for both binding and illumination) of 76 florins 15 soldi and 11 denars. The illustrations displayed include images of Pliny as the scholarly scientist; and Filippo Strozzi and his son (lower right). The coat of arms in the lower margin is that of Filippo (in his accounts Strozzi referred to this book as 'my Pliny'), between two representations of the Strozzi emblem (a lamb lying in a field, with the motto 'Mitis Esto'). At the beginning of each book of the *Natural history* is a beautifully decorated historiated initial, illustrating the subject of the book.

In addition to being sumptuously illuminated, this book is also elegantly bound: the binding is of blind-tooled dark olive-green goatskin over wooden boards; the large silver catches on the lower cover bear the emblem of the Strozzi and their motto. The silver ornaments which secured the now missing clasps bear the arms of the de Nobili family: Giulio d'Antonio de Nobili owned the book in the 16th century. Thereafter, no information is known about its history until it became part of the collection of Francis Douce (1757–1834), Keeper of Manuscripts in the British Museum Library, which passed, on his death, to the Bodleian. Douce's bequest consisted of more than 19,000 printed volumes alone, including 479 incunables. These filled many gaps in the Bodleian's collections, for Douce collected many items, such as literature in the vernacular, fables and romances, sermons and preaching manuals—not the type of material the Library had purchased at, for example, the Pinelli or Crevenna sales.

Bequeathed, 1834. *Douce 310* [kept as *Arch. G b.6*], *fol. [a]6r*

The Douce legacy: an exhibition to commemorate the 150th anniversary of the bequest of Francis Douce (1757-1834). (Oxford: Bodleian Library, 1984). No. 129.

The painted page: Italian Renaissance book illumination, 1450-1550. Ed. by Jonathan J. G. Alexander (Munich, 1994). No. 85 (with references).

LIBRO PRIMO DELLA NATVRALE HISTORIA DI .C.
PLINIO SECONDO TRADOCTA IN LINGVA FIOREN
TINA PER CHRISTOPHORO LANDINO FIORENTI
NO AL SERENISSIMO FERDINANDO RE DI NAPOLI.
PREFATIONE

ITERMINAI O GIOCONDISSIMO
imperadore con epistola forse di troppa licétia
narrarti elibri della historia naturale: opera no
uella alle muse romane: nata appresso di me nel
lultima genitura. Sia adunq; questa prefatiõe
uerissima di te métre che gia inuecchia nel grã
dissimo tuo padre : per che usando el uerso di
Catullo mio compatriota tu soleui pure stima
re qualche chosa le mie ciácie. Tu conosci que
sta castrense & militare parola. Et lui chome tu
sai mutando le prime syllabe si fece alquanto
piu duro che non uolea essere stimato da tuoi
familiari & serui . Per questo adunq; ditermi
nai scriuerti: & áchora per che le nostre chose apparischino & sieno manifeste p questa
mia audacia maxime dolédoti tu che pel passato non lhabbi facto in una altra nostra
procace epistola. Et accio che tutti glhuomini sappino quanto di pari lomperio techo
uiua: Tu elquale hai triomphato & se stato censore & sei uolte cósolo & participe del
la tribunitia potesta: Se stato prefecto del pretorio:ilche hai facto piu nobile che tutti
glaltri magistrati:perche per piacere a tuo padre & allordine equestre lacceptasti : Et
tutte queste cose per rispecto della republica hai facto : Et me chome nel contubernio
castrense tractasti ? Et certo niéte ha mutato inte lamplitudine & grandezza della tua
fortuna:se non che tanto piu possi & uogla giouare:quáto quella e maggiore. Adũq;
bêche a tutti glaltri huomini sia aperta la uia a impetrare ogni chosa da te uenerádoti:
Niente di meno solo laudacia fa che io piu familiarmente te honori. Questa audacia
adunq; imputerai a te medesimo:& a te medesimo nel nostro fallo perdonerai.Io mi
stroppicciai la faccia:& niente di meno nessuno proficto ho facto: perche per unaltra
uia mapparisti grande:& di lontano mi rimuoui con le faccelline del tuo ingegno . Et
certo in nexuno piu sfolgora quella:laquale piu uerámente e decta in te che in altri for
za deloquentia. In te e quella facundia che alla tribunitia potesta si conuiene:Con qta
risonantia tuoni tu le laude paterne? Có quanta(non sanza amore)dimostri quelle di
tuo fratello? Quanto se excellente & sublime nella poetica faculta ? O gran fecondita
danimo. Certo hai trouato inche modo possi imitare tuo fratello . Ma queste chose
chi potrebbe sanza paura considerare : hauendo a uenire al giudicio dellongegno
tuo : maxime essendo quello dame prouocato ? Certamente non sono in simile
conditione quegli che publicano alchuno libro:& quegli che ate glintitolano. Impero
che se io lo publicassi & non lo intitolassi ate:potrei dire perche leggi tu queste chose o
imperadore:lequali sono scripte albasso uulgo & alla turba de glagricultori & de glar
tefici & a quegli che cósumano elloro otio negli studii?Perche adunq; ti fa tu giudice:
concio sia che quando io scriueuo questa opera:non thaueuo posto nella tauola doue
sono descripti egiudici?Et eri di tanta excellentia ? che non stimauo che tu ti degnassi
scendere si basso?Pretera quando bene non fussi in si excelso grado:nientedimeno gli
scriptori comunemente fuggono el giudicio de docti . Questo fa Cicerone:elquale e
di tanta eloquentia:che puo sottomettere longegno al giuocho della fortuna : & quel

26 Aulus Gellius, *Noctes Atticae*. [Rome:] In Domo Petri de Maximis (Conrad Sweynheym & Arnold Pannartz), 11 Apr. 1469.

The 'Attic Nights' of Aulus Gellius (fl. *c*.125/8–180 AD) are so-called from the fact that Gellius began to collect the material for them during the long winter nights of a visit to Greece, where he listened to conversations, which, added to what he read, subsequently became a collection of essays in twenty books. They cover a wide variety of subjects, including history, law, philosophy, and grammar. Much read in late Antiquity, excerpts of the 'Attic Nights' were included in several medieval florilegia, and, during the Renaissance, Gellius' work was seen as a model of humanist writing.

It was presumably for this reason that Gellius attracted the interest of the early printers: ten incunable editions were printed. This copy is of the first edition, printed by two Germans, Conrad Sweynheym and Arnold Pannartz. In 1463, they set up the first printing press outside Germany, at Subiaco, near Rome. However, they moved into Rome itself during 1467. In 1472, in an application to Pope Sixtus IV, the two Germans stated that they usually printed 275 copies of each edition.

The page illustrated shows fine contemporary illumination, with a Roman initial letter 'P' in gilt. The first known owner of this book was Maffeo Pinelli (1735–1785), the hereditary Director of the official Venetian Press. Pinelli had inherited what has been described as 'one of the great libraries of classical literature in fine Italian printing'. After his death, his books were bought by the London bookseller, James Edwards, and sold at auction.

For the Bodleian the 1789 Pinelli sale was a particular landmark in the development of its collections, in that it saw the beginning of a concerted policy of purchasing first or early editions of the Latin and Greek classical authors. By the middle of the eighteenth century, the original Bodleian endowment (which included money for purchasing books) was being used almost in its entirety to pay for the running of the Library, and there was little money left for the purchase of new books: indeed, by the 1730s, only about £7 per annum was being spent on books. The situation improved a little in 1750, when money left to the Library in 1721 by Lord Crewe finally became available, thus guaranteeing a sum of £10 annually for the purchase of books. The deficiencies in

the Bodleian's collections became ever more apparent, and drew considerable criticism, but, initially, no extra financial support. Eventually, a proposal promoted by William Scot, Camden Professor of Ancient History, led to the transfer of certain University fees to the Library, thereby vastly increasing the purchasing budget to some £400. Although this did allow gaps to be filled, there were still critical remarks about book selection being 'neither rational nor efficient'. One especially fierce attack, from the incoming Reader in Chemistry, Thomas Lovell Beddoes, in 1787, led the Curators of the Bodleian to institute new procedures, whereby they would meet regularly to order the purchase of books, and examine booksellers' catalogues. Thus, by the time of the Pinelli sale in 1789, the Library was comparatively well placed to respond to this wonderful opportunity. Two of the Curators, John Randolph, Regius Professor of Divinity, and William Jackson, Regius Professor of Greek, were commissioned to decide on purchases to be made at the sale, and to arrange for bids to be placed. Their selections were, presumably, influenced by the recent decision to make the newly established 'Auctarium' (formerly the Anatomy School, and now the main enquiry room in the Lower Reading Room) the repository for the Library's Greek and Biblical manuscripts and 15th-century classical texts, ready for collation for the new editions which would then be published by the University Press (of which both Jackson and Randolph were also Curators).

The bidding was highly successful, and the Bodleian acquired more than 70 incunables (costing in excess of £500), including the Gellius displayed here. However, this left the Bodleian's account in deficit—by approximately £500. The Curators issued a notice to all members of the University notifying them of the Library's intention 'to borrow either from Colleges or Individuals such Sums of Money, as they may be disposed to offer ...' Despite the conflict between the Curators (who wished to see money spent on 'new books') and Heads of Houses who were more interested in longer opening hours and better services, the appeal was answered handsomely, to the tune of £1600. Having acquired so many magnificent books at Pinelli's sale, the Library then set about having them rebound suitably. The Bodleian commissioned two

Lutarchus in libro qué ο ποσῃ ψυ χωρ και
σωματων αυθρωποισ περι ενφυιαυ και
αρετηυ διαφορα. id est quantū inter hoíes
animi corpisq; ingēio atq; uirtutibus intersit:
conscripsit: scite subtyliterq; ratiocinatum Py/
thagoram philosophum dicit: in reperienda:
moduládaq; status lógitudinis eius p̄stantia.
Nam quum fere cōstaret curriculum stadii: quod est Pisis: apud
Iouem Olympium: Herculem pedibus suis metatum: id q; fecisse
longū pedes ducentos: cetera quoq; stadia in terris grecie ab aliis
postea instituta: pedum quidem esse numero ducentorum: sed tñ
esse aliquátulum breuiora: facile intellexit: modū spatiū q; plāte
Herculis: róe proportóis habita: tanto fuisse q̄ aliorum pcerius:
quanto olympicum stadium longius esset q̄ cetera. Comprehensa
autem mensura herculani pedis: secundū naturalem membrorum
omniū inter se competentiā modificatus est. Atq; ita id collegit:
quod erat cōsequens: táto fuisse Herculem corpore excelliorē q̄
alios: q̄nto olympicū stadiū ceteris pari numero factis anteiret.

Ab Herode Attico cōsulari uiro tempestiue deprompta in
quendam iactatum & gloriosum adolescētem: specie tantū
philosophie sectatorē uerba Epicteti stoici: q̄bus festiuiter
a uero stoico seiúxit uulgus loquacium nebulonum: qui se
stoicos nuncuparent. Caput .ii.

Herodes Atticus uir & greca facundia & consulari honore
p̄reditus: accersebat sepe nos: quum apud magistros athenis
essemus: í uillas eius urbi p̄ximas: me & clarissimū uirū Seruilianū:
complurisq; alios nostrates: qui roma in grecíam: ad capiendum
ingenii cultum cōcesserant. Atq; ibi tunc quum essemus apud eū
in uilla cui nomē est Cephysia: & estu āni: & sidere autumni fla/
grātissimo: propulsabamus caloris incommoda: lucorum umbra
ingentiū longis ābulacris: & mollibus: ediū posticū refrigerātibus
lauacris nitidis: & abundis: & collucētibus: totiusq; uille uenustate

German binders, working in London, Heinrich Walther and Christian Samuel Kalthoeber, to bind the books in plain red morocco. The Gellius was bound by Walther, and is stamped on both covers with the gilt Bodleian stamp, which had been engraved in 1789 especially for this purpose.

Purchased, 1789. *Auct. L 2.2, fol. [b]1r*

Alan Coates, 'The Bodleian's incunabula in the late eighteenth and nineteenth centuries: their acquisition, cataloguing and housing', *The Bodleian Library Record*, 15/2 (1995), 108-18.

Kristian Jensen, 'Heinrich Walther, Christian Samuel Kalthoeber and other London binders: books in the Bodleian Library bound by Germans settled in London in the eighteenth century', *Bibliothek und Wissenschaft*, 29 (1996), 292-311.

Ian Philip, 'The background to Bodleian purchases of incunabula at the Pinelli and Crevenna sales 1789-90', *Transactions of the Cambridge Bibliographical Society*, 7 (1979), 369-75.

27 Plutarchus, *Vitae illustrium virorum*. Venice: Nicolaus Jenson, 2 Jan. 1478.

This edition of the 'Lives of Famous Men' by the Greek writer Plutarch (*c.*46–120 AD) was printed by the well-known Venetian printer Nicolaus Jenson. The text was originally written in Greek, as a series of parallel lives, one from ancient Greek history, the other from Roman history. These were later translated into Latin by several Italian humanists. In addition they translated works by other Greek authors (such as Isocrates and Xenophon), to supplement Plutarch's corpus, and these were often simply attributed to him as well; the humanists also added works of their own (for example, the lives of Aristotle and Charlemagne), and of other authors, such as the 'Life of Atticus' by Nepos, and the 'Roman history' by a rather problematical author, who goes under a variety of name forms, including Festus Rufius.

The printer, Jenson, described by one modern writer as 'one of the greatest type-designers of all time', was, by profession, a die-cutter from Troyes: according to tradition, he was sent by King Charles VII of France to Mainz to spy on printing which was taking place there—surely one of the earliest examples of what would now be deemed industrial espionage. Jenson seems to have learned to print in Germany, perhaps in Mainz, before settling in Venice, where he was certainly in residence by 1470. William Morris declared that 'Jenson carried the development of roman type as far as it can go', and it is easy to identify with such opinions when observing the elegant and well-crafted letters in this beautiful type.

The earliest known provenance of this rather grand copy is Italian, as shown by the characteristic vine-stem decoration. The contemporary episcopal coat of arms has not been identified. Subsequently, the book passed into two aristocratic collections. The first was Italian, that of Prince Vincenzo Carafa (died 1814). The second was British, that of the Dukes of Sutherland—it was probably acquired by George Leveson-Gower, 2nd Duke of Sutherland (1786–1861), and his coat of arms, encircled by the Garter, is stamped in gilt on the elegant red morocco binding. This book is an example of a recent acquisition of rare books by the Bodleian, exemplifying the Library's commitment to a continuing policy of collecting. It was part of the gift of Miriam Robinette Tomkinson (1916–1986), a member of a book-collecting Worcestershire family, who was herself the great-great niece of Ingram Bywater (1840–1914), former Regius Professor of Greek, Bodleian Sub-Librarian and Library benefactor. The majority of the books, both those presented and those later bequeathed by Tomkinson, are classical texts, and they were added by the Bodleian to the collection left by Bywater himself, as contributing to the history of classical scholarship.

Presented, 1984. *Byw. adds. 2, fol. a2r*

G[eoffrey] G[room], 'Notable accessions', *Bodleian Library Record*, 12/2 (1986), 145-7.

Martin Lowry, *Nicolaus Jenson and the rise of Venetian publishing in Renaissance Europe* (Oxford: Blackwell, 1991), *ad indicem*.

S.H. Steinberg, *Five hundred years of printing*. New ed., revised by John Trevitt (London: British Library, 1996), *ad indicem*.

THESEI VITA PER LAPVM FLORENTINVM EX PLVTARCO GRAECO IN LATINVM VERSA.

QVEMADMODVM IN ORBIS TERRAE situ defcribendo hiftorici folent: ut ad quæ ipfi cognitione afpirare non poffunt: extremis tabularū partibus fupprimentes quibufdam adiiciunt locos effe uaftos arenofos & cælo terraq; penuriam aquarum: aut limum infuperabilem: aut mōtem ftiticum: aut aftrictum frigore pontum: ita & nobis in hac uirorum collatione perpetua rerū hiftoria quantū probabili oratione affequi potuimus: de his quos fupra memorauimus uiris tempora percurrētibus uere licuit affirmare. Quæ uero antiquiora ac uetuftiora funt: tragica & monftruofa poetæ & fabulofi rerum fcriptores occupant: nec ultra fidem ullam nec certitudinem præfe ferunt. Cum igitur Lycurgi legū latoris & Nume regis res geftas litteris mandauerimus: haud ab re tuerit ad Romulum orationem conuertere: quando hiftoria ipfa ad eius tempora q̄ prope acceffimus. Sed mihi diu cogitāti huic uiro (ut inquit Aefchilus) quis conueniret: quem illi opponerem: quis dignus fecum in comparatione cōiungi: ufum eft tandem faciendum effe: ut a quo celebrata Athenienfium ciuitas amplificata eft: eum cum gloriofiffimæ atq; inuictiffimæ urbis Romæ parente conferrem & compararem. Licet autem nobis reiectis fabulis ad ipfam claram hiftoriæ lucem & ueritatem accedere. Quod ficubi neceffitas coget nos ab hac parumper digreffos: ad id quod uerifimile fit conferre: a quo fortaffe hiftoria abhorreat: nec admittat ullum cū probabilitate cōmertium: æquis auditoribus opus erit: quiq; benigne & humane initium orationis exaudiant atq; approbent. Videtur igitur Thefeus multis de caufis Romulo q̄fimillimus extitiffe. Ambo .n. cum fpurii & obfcuri forent: exiftimati funt a Diis imortalibus procreati effe. Ambo ét belicofi ac manu ftrenui: hoc quidem omnes fcimus: & quanta maxime fieri potuit prudētia præftiterunt. ex duabus quoq; clariffimis ciuitatibus Roma & Athenis: alteram hic condidit: alteram ille nouis colonis compleuit. Fœminarum præterea raptus de utroq; feruntur: nec eorum quifq̄ domefticam cladem & crimina fuorum effugit: fed ad poftremum ambo dicuntur in inuidiam & offenfionem ciuium incidiffe. Siquid igitur ex his quæ minus tragice dici uidentur ad ueritatem conducit: Thefei quidem paternum genus in erechtheum ac primos indigenas referebatur: maternum uero in Pelopem. Pelops enim non opibus magis & copiis q̄ natorum fobole cæterorum Peloponefi regum potentiffimus fuit: cū filias permultas optimatibus in matrimonio locaffet: multofq; in rebufp. paffim principes difperfiffet: e quibus unus Pittheus extitit Thefei maternus auus: qui urbem nō magnam trœzeniorum incoluit: is qui per id temporis omnibus fapientia & eloquentia plurimum præftare putabatur. Fuit eius fapientiæ ut uidetur talis quædam uis ac forma: qualem complexus Hefiodus cum fua fcripta fententiis plurimis referfiffet: fapiens imprimis eft habitus: atq; eam unam ex Pitthei fententiis fuiffe memorant: Efto fatis comiti merces promiffa laboris. Cuius rei Ariftoteles philofophus ē auctor. Euripides etiam cum Hippolytum cafti Pitthei difciplinam appellet: hanc eandē de Pittheo opinionem perfpicue atteftari uidetur. Aegeo uero cum filiis indigeret: uulgatum illud oraculum Pythiam uatem ceciniffe ferūt: quo iuffit ne cum muliere coiret: priufq̄ Athenas accederet. quod cum non fatis aperte dixiffe uideretur: in Trœzenem profectus: de Dei refponfo cum Pittheo communicauit: quod huiufmodi fuit: Neue

a 2

Comparatio thefei et Romuli.

De gñe thefei
Pelops

Pittheus

N

Aegeus

28 Aesopus, *Vita et fabulae*, trans. William Caxton (Westminster: William Caxton, 26 Mar. 1484).

Aesop's *Fables* probably originated in the 5th century BC, with a Greek slave of that name, who gained a reputation as a teller of animal stories. Over the succeeding years, the corpus of fables was expanded, to include those of other writers, such as Phaedrus and Avianus. The invention of printing saw a further increase in the popularity of these works, with more than 150 editions being printed before 1500 in a wide range of languages (Greek, Latin, German, French, Italian, Dutch, Czech, Spanish, and English). The *Fables* became a standard school-text throughout Europe during the Renaissance, but were also used for the moral instruction of adults.

This edition of the *Fables* was translated by William Caxton from the French collection of fables put together by Julian Macho; Macho's version was, itself, derived from that of Heinrich Steinhoewel. Caxton's edition contains 167 fables and a *Life* of Aesop: these fables include six tales not in the Steinhoewel or Macho collections, but omit three included by Steinhoewel, thus well illustrating the adjustments made by each compiler of such collections. The opening displayed shows the fables of the rat and the dog, and the dog and the sheep, illustrated by two of the 186 woodcuts which appear in this edition: these were copied (by Caxton's artist) from a well-known series of designs for illustrations for the Aesop stories, which had first been used in Johann Zainer's Ulm edition of *c.*1476–7.

This copy is the last item in a volume containing four works printed by William Caxton (*c.*1420–1491), the mercer who introduced printing to England in 1476, when he returned from Bruges and established his press at Westminster: he has been described as 'probably the best-known and most widely honored Englishman of his century'. In this copy the similarity of the hands in which notes and names are written in all four items suggests that they were travelling together from at least the early 16th century. Today the book is bound in 19th-century calf, in a binding made for the Bodleian Library and bearing its gilt stamp on both covers. The volume seems to have been used by several 16th-century English owners, including one Richard Story, who describes himself as 'citizen and fishmonger of London'. It then seems to have passed into the hands of Gisbert Voetius (1588–1676), the Dutch theologian and Professor of Divinity at Utrecht, and later to the London publisher, Moses Pitt (fl. 1654–1696). The first volume of Pitt's *English atlas* appeared in 1680, the year he gave this copy of Aesop to the Bodleian. Pitt was clearly a well-known figure in Oxford, and had numerous acquaintances here, including Dr. Fell at Christ Church, and Obadiah Walker, Master of University College; and the four volumes of the *Atlas*, which were eventually produced, were all printed in the Sheldonian Theatre. It is, therefore, not surprising that he should have chosen to present such an important volume as the Aesop to the Bodleian Library.

Presented, 1680. *Arch. G d.13(4), fols. d8v–e1r*

Caxton's Aesop. Ed. with introduction and notes by R.T. Lenaghan (Cambridge, Mass.: Harvard UP, 1967).

Liber primus

¶ The thyrd fable is of the rat/and of the frogge/

Now it be so/ that as the rat wente in pylgrymage/ he came by a Ryuer/ and demaunded helpe of a frogge for to passe/ and go ouer the water/ And thenne the frogge bounde the rats foote to her foote/ and thus swymmed vnto the myddes ouer the Ryuer/ And as they were there the frogge stoode stylle/ to thende that the rat sholde be drowned/ And in the meane whyle came a kyte vpon them/ and bothe bare them with hym/ This fable made Esope for a symplytude whiche is prouffitable to many folkes/ For he that thynketh euylle ageynst good/the euylle whiche he thynketh shall ones falle vpon hym self

¶ The fourth fable is of the dogge and of the sheep

Of the men chalengynge/whiche euer be settynge occasion to doo some harme and dommage to the good/ sayth Esope such a fable/ Somtyme was a dogge/whiche

demaunded of a sheep a loof of bred that she had borowed of hym/ And the sheep ansuerd that neuer she had none of hym/ The dogge made her to come before the Iuge/ And by cause the sheep denyed the dette/ the dogge prouysed and broughte with hym fals wytnes/ that is to wete the wulf/ the mylan & the sperehawke/ And whanne these wytnes sholde be examyned and herd/ the wulf sayd to the Iuge/I am certayne & me remembreth wel/ that the dogge lend to her a loof of bred And the Myllan went and sayd/ she wayued hit presente my persone/ And the sperowhauke sayd to the sheep/ Come hyder why denyest thow that whiche thow hast take and wayued/ And thus was the poure sheep vanquysshed/ ¶ And thenne the Iuge commaunded to her that she sholde paye the dogge/Wherfore she sold awey before the wynter her flees and wulle for to paye that/that she neuer had/ And thus was the poure sheep despoylled/In suche maner done the euylle hongry peple whiche by theyr grete vntrouthe and malyce robben and despoyllen the poure folke

¶ The fyfthe fable is of the dogge and of the pyere of flessh

e i

29 *The book of hawking, hunting and heraldry*. Westminster: Wynkyn de Worde, 1496.

The 'Treatyse of fysshynge with an Angle', the opening page of which is here illustrated, appears in the second edition of the *Book of hawking, hunting and heraldry*. It has been traditionally, but incorrectly, ascribed to 'Dame Juliana Berners'. Her name is found at the end of the treatise on hunting: she has been tentatively identified with Juliana Berners (fl. 1460), Prioress of Sopwell Nunnery, near St. Albans.

The claim made by one writer in 1910 that the treatise on fishing was 'not only the first angling manual in England, but … also the first practical work of the kind written in any language' cannot now be sustained (it was Aelfric in the 10th century who wrote the earliest description in English of fishing). In spite of this, the treatise was of considerable importance as the first printed manual on the subject in English.

The work begins with an eloquent plea for angling. This is followed by lessons in the manufacture of fishing rods, lines and hooks. The methods of catching fish, including the best places, times of day and weather are all discussed, along with types of bait.

The printer, Wynkyn de Worde, came from Alsace. He became William Caxton's apprentice soon after the latter set up his press at Westminster, and may, indeed, have come over with him from Bruges. On Caxton's death in *c.*1491, Wynkyn took over Caxton's press, and continued to use his former master's old types until at least 1493. Whereas Caxton had been both an editor and translator, in addition to being a printer, Wynkyn was really more of a businessman, who concentrated on printing and selling books. When he died in 1535, he had published some 600 books, thus making him 'the most prolific of all the early English printers'.

This copy had various early west country owners, including John Vowell or Hooker (1527–1601), a Member of Parliament, and the City Chamberlain of Exeter; and George Carew, Earl of Totnes (1555–1629), whose coat of arms is stamped on the 17th-century parchment binding. Both of these men would have known Thomas Bodley. The book was subsequently owned by John Selden (1584–1654), the lawyer, antiquary, Member of Parliament and book collector, whose splendid collection of some 8,000 volumes remains (after that of Francis Douce) one of the most significant ever given to the Bodleian, both in terms of its size, and its breadth, showing the range of Selden's own interests in law, languages, history, and antiquities. With the exception of early English imprints such as this, it seems unlikely that Selden collected incunabula for their age or rarity, and the majority of his more than one hundred incunabula fall within the range of his general academic interests.

Presented, 1659. *S. Seld. d.17(1), fol. g3v*

Dame Juliana Berners, *A treatyse of fysshynge wyth an angle*. With introduction by M.G. Watkins (London: Elliot Stock, 1880).
W.L. Braekman, *The treatise on angling in 'The boke of St. Albans' (1496)*, Scripta 1 (Brussels, 1980).

Here begynnyth the treatyse of fysshynge wyth an Angle.

Alamon in his parablys sayth that a good spyryte makyth a flourynge aege) that is a fayre aege & a longe. And syth it is soo: I aske this questyon) whiche ben the meanes & the causes that enduce a man in to a mery spyryte.: Truly to my beste dyscrecōn it semeth good dysportes & honest gamps in whom a man Joyeth wythout ony repentannce after. Thenne folowyth it ꝑ gode dysportes & honest games ben cause of mannys fayr aege & longe life. And therfore now woll I chose of foure good dysportes & honeste gamps) that is to wyte: of huntynge: hawkynge: fysshynge: & foulynge. The beste to my symple dyscrecōn whyche is fysshynge: callyd Anglynge wyth a rodde: and a lyne

30 Bernhard von Breydenbach, *Peregrinatio in terram sanctam*. Mainz: Erhard Reuwich, 11 Feb. 1486.

Bernhard von Breydenbach (died 1497) became Canon of Mainz in 1450. To ensure the salvation of his soul, Breydenbach resolved to go on pilgrimage to the Holy Land. Among those who accompanied him was Erhard Reuwich, an artist from Utrecht. Reuwich both printed the account of the journey, and made the drawings from which the illustrations in the book were produced.

Breydenbach is described as author of the *Peregrinatio* (although the Latin text was probably compiled by Martin Roth, a Dominican from Pforzheim): the work is the earliest printed 'tourist guide'. It contains maps, of which this view of Venice is one of the grandest. The culmination of the trip (with the largest map) is the Holy Land. The book also contains historical information (accounts of various sieges of places along the route, such as that of Constantinople in 1453), a vocabulary of 228 Arabic words translated into Latin and other languages, and remedies for sea sickness.

The pilgrims left Mainz on 25 April 1483, and took 15 days to reach Venice. A description of relics seen in Venice is provided, such as an arm of St. George, a thumb of the Emperor Constantine, and one of the six jars in which water was turned to wine at Cana. The party stayed 22 days at Venice, giving Reuwich time to make sketches for the view of the city: the opening on display here is probably taken from where S. Giorgio Maggiore now stands, with the Campanile and Doges' Palace prominent in the foreground. The pilgrims left Venice on 1 June, and reached Jerusalem on 11 July. An account of the places visited by the pilgrims in the Holy Land is given, and a description of the area and the inhabitants. The party finally returned to Venice on 8 January 1484.

The first known owner of the book was Pietro-Antonio Bolongaro-Crevenna (1735–1792). Crevenna came from Italy, but subsequently became a trader in snuff in Amsterdam, and put together a splendid library, which he intended to use as material for a work on the history of printing (a project begun but never finished). The bulk of the collection was sold in 1790. The Crevenna sale is interesting from a Bodleian perspective because the Library continued the process started at the Pinelli sale, of buying early editions of classical texts, and, indeed, bought even more heavily in 1790 than in 1789, with the Library spending more than £1000. Such was the expense that the Library was faced with a debt of more than £1500, although careful financial management, allowed the debts to be cleared by 1795. At the Crevenna sale, this book was purchased by Francis Douce (1757-1834).

Bequeathed, 1834. *Douce 223,* [kept as *Arch. B c.25*], *fold-out map of Venice.*

Hugh W. Davies, *Bernhard von Breydenbach and his journey to the Holy Land 1483–4.* (London, 1911).

Alan Coates, 'The Bodleian's incunabula in the late eighteenth and nineteenth centuries: their acquisition, cataloguing and housing', *The Bodleian Library Record*, 15/2 (1995), 108–18.

The Douce legacy: an exhibition to commemorate the 150th anniversary of the bequest of Francis Douce (1757-1834) (Oxford: Bodleian Library, 1984).

Ian Philip, 'The background to Bodleian purchases of incunabula at the Pinelli and Crevenna sales 1789–90', *Transactions of the Cambridge Bibliographical Society*, 7 (1979), 369–75.

69

The music collections

31-37

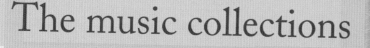

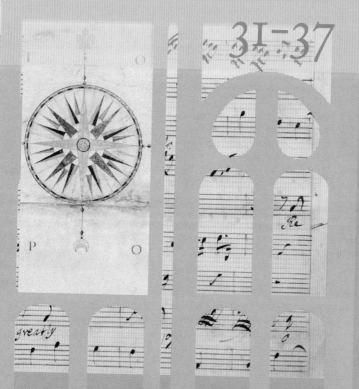

31   William Lawes (1602–1645), Music for viols and organ

2002 is also the quatercentenary of the birth of William Lawes, a brilliant and original composer, especially of music for viol consort, who served as a royal musician to Charles I. It is not certain whether Lawes came to Oxford with the court in 1642, but if so, he soon left to become a soldier in the royal cause, and was killed three years later at the Siege of Chester in September 1645. This volume is one of a pair, and bears the royal arms on the front cover together with the composer's initials WL. Its companion has the initials HL, and must have originally belonged to his elder brother, Henry, also in royal service. Henry did not use his own volume, but evidently gave it to the prolific William to fill. The two volumes contain probably the earliest substantial quantity of music of any composer to have survived in his own hand. Most manuscript music from before this period is found only in scribal copies, not in a composer's autograph. The page shows music for two bass viols and organ, where the energy of Lawes's writing seems almost to spring from the page. The volumes (together with a set of separate partbooks also in William's hand) were apparently presented or bequeathed by Henry Lawes to the Oxford Music School collection, probably through John Wilson, a fellow member of the King's musicians, who was professor of music at Oxford from 1656 to 1661.

The Music School collection had its origins in a gift of printed and manuscript music from William Heather, a Gentleman of the Chapel Royal, in 1627. This contained fine sets of printed madrigals and motets, as well an important set of mid-16th century partbooks of music by John Taverner and others. He also endowed what was to become the music professorship, as well as giving instruments, all with the intention of promoting musical activity in the University. The Music School had its home in the Schools quadrangle (where one doorway still bears the name 'Schola Musicae' above it), and the collection was added to through the 17th and 18th centuries, particularly with consort music, printed Italian instrumental music, and the complete court odes of William Boyce. The collection was transferred to the Bodleian in 1885.

Presented to the Music School, c.1660, transferred to the Bodleian, 1885. *MS. Mus. Sch. B 2, p. 93*

72

Paven. and 2 Almans of Alfonso. sett to the Organ
and 2 division Basstviolls by M. W. Lawes

32 The Earliest Engraved Music in England

***Parthenia or The maydenhead of the first
musicke that ever was printed for the virginalls***.
(London, G. Lowe, [*c*.1613].)

This collection of music for the virginals (a member of
the harpsichord family) contains works by three famous
composers of the day, William Byrd, John Bull and
Orlando Gibbons, and the title-page purports to show
St. Cecilia seated at the instrument. In the 17th century
engraving music on copper plates was the only practical
method of printing keyboard music, since typeset music
(usual for vocal music at this time) could not cope with
its complexities of layout. The expense of engraving on
copper, however, meant that little keyboard music was
in fact printed before the end of the century, when the introduction of cheaper pewter plates made it economically
feasible. *Parthenia* was first issued with a leaf of dedication to Frederick, the Elector Palatine and his 'betrothed'
Lady Elizabeth, daughter of King James I, presumably
before their wedding on 24 February 1613. It was then

reissued with the words 'Dedicated to all the Maisters
and Lovers of Musick' added to the title-page, and a
changed imprint. The Bodleian's copy is of this reissue,
and was received by February 1614 under the terms of Sir
Thomas Bodley's 1610 agreement with the Stationers'
Company. Only a few other musical publications of the
time were likewise received, but they do include some
extremely rare items, including one of only two recorded
copies of John Maynard's *The XII wonders of the world*
(London, 1611). British music began to arrive on a regular
basis under legal deposit only from about 1780, seemingly
prompted by a series of court cases, which had confirmed
that intellectual copyright could reside in items other
than ordinary printed books. Since that time music of all
types, classical and popular, has flowed into the Library,
although until the early 20th century the deposit of music
continued to be somewhat haphazard, with some publishers sending everything and others nothing.

Presented by the Stationers' Company, 1614. *Arch. A c.11*

PARTHENIA

or

THE MAYDENHEAD

of the first musicke that

euer was printed for the VIRGINALLS.

COMPOSED

By three famous Masters: William Byrd, Dr: John Bull, & Orlando Gibbons,
Gentilmen of his Ma:ties most Illustrious Chappell.

Dedicated to all the Maisters and Louers of Musick.

Ingrauen

by William Hole.

for

DORETHIE EUANS.

Cum

Priuilegio.

Printed at LONDON by G: Lowe and are to be soulde
at his howse in Loathberry.

33 Henry Purcell (1659–1695),
Autograph manuscript of the Ode for St. Cecilia's Day, 1692.

Annual London celebrations in honour of the patron saint of music on her name day, 22 November, were instituted in 1683, and included the performance of an ode in praise of music. Purcell composed at least twice for the occasion, and his richly scored 1692 work, 'Hail, bright Cecilia', to words by Nicholas Brady extolling the virtues of instruments and voices, is one of his grandest and finest works. The composer's characteristically rather rough working score shows here the countertenor air ''Tis Nature's voice', with its extravagantly ornamented vocal line. Purcell's score unfortunately suffered early physical neglect, which led to the total loss of the first five leaves (containing the Overture), which were replaced in early 18th-century manuscript, as well as damage to other leaves. The manuscript came to the Bodleian in 1801 under the bequest of Osborne Wight, Fellow of New College, who allowed the Library to select whatever items of his collection of printed and manuscript music it desired. The Bodleian thus acquired much fine 17th- and 18th-century English music, including autograph works of William Croft, Maurice Greene and William Boyce as well as those of Oxford musicians like William and Philip Hayes, and 18th-century printed editions of Handel and others. The acquisition really laid the foundations of the Library's post-medieval music manuscript collection, which hitherto had comprised only a solitary 17th-century volume of the songs of John Wilson, presented by the composer himself in 1656.

Bequeathed, 1801. *MS. Mus. c. 26, fol. 38r*

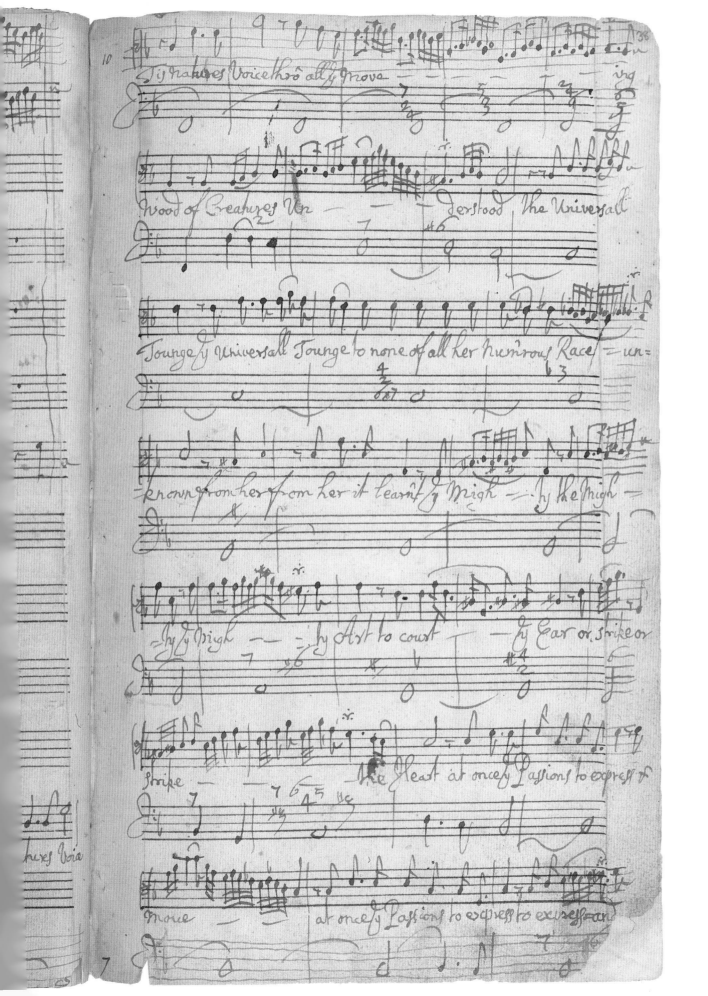

34 Handel's Own Conducting Score of *Messiah*

This is the score of George Frideric Handel's most famous oratorio from which the composer conducted the first performance in Dublin (1743) and all subsequent ones in which he was involved. It is not the original composing score (now in the British Library), but the first copy made from it by Handel's principal copyist, John Christopher Smith. Into it Handel himself not only inserted performance markings, but also alternative versions of certain arias. One such, shown here, is the now familiar version of 'Rejoice greatly', which replaced an earlier version in 12/8 time. Handel here first had Smith write out the bass line, which remained unchanged from the earlier version; the composer then filled in the new version of the vocal and violin lines above. Throughout the score Handel also noted the names of singers on the various occasions. This aria, for example, was sung by the famous soprano Giulia Frasi, as well as (unusually) by a tenor, John Beard, and by an anonymous treble, 'The boy'.

The provenance history of the score (which is in two volumes) is incomplete, but it appeared in the sale-room in 1838, when it was bought for one guinea. It later passed to E.J. Ottley, who presented it to Sir Frederick Gore Ouseley in 1867. Ouseley, who was Heather Professor of Music at Oxford from 1855, founded St. Michael's College, Tenbury in the following year, intending it to be a model institution for the cultivation of cathedral-style worship, which it successfully proved to be for well over a century. Ouseley's very fine music library was bequeathed to the College, though with the proviso that it should come to the Bodleian in the event of the college's closure. When that came about in 1985, legal complications precluded a gift of the entire collection, but with the amicable agreement of the Trustees of St. Michael's the manuscripts were donated, whilst the Bodleian purchased such books and printed music as were not already in its collections. With over one thousand manuscripts, the acquisition of the Tenbury collection almost doubled the number of music manuscripts in the Bodleian, with great strengths in Tudor and Jacobean partbooks, and 18th-century Italian opera scores, as well as including autograph manuscripts of, amongst others, John Blow, Johann Pachelbel, Johann Christian Bach, Baldassare Galuppi and Domenico Cimarosa.

Presented, 1985. *MS. Tenbury 346, fol. 66r*

35 Felix Mendelssohn Bartholdy, Autograph score of the *Hebrides* Overture

Mendelssohn's *Hebrides* or *Fingal's Cave* Overture was inspired by a visit to Scotland in 1829, which included a trip to Staffa. It was nearly three years in gestation, and this score, full of revisions, is the composer's final working manuscript of the piece, dated at the end, London, 20 June 1832. Mendelssohn himself presented it to his English friend William Sterndale Bennett in 1837, and it descended in that family to the present day. It was purchased at auction in May 2002, thanks to generous funding from the Heritage Lottery Fund, the Friends of the Bodleian and many supporters. It joins other material related to the work in the Library's magnificent Mendelssohn collection, which includes the only drawing that Mendelssohn made of the Hebrides, an early draft of the score in a copyist's hand, and the

composer's autograph arrangement for piano duet. The Mendelssohn collection was acquired largely by donation (directly and indirectly) from descendants of the composer between 1960 and 1974. It is particularly strong on biographical material, including most of the letters received by the composer, student notes, books of drawings, diaries, albums, and much of his musical library. Besides the *Hebrides*, other important musical autographs are those of the organ sonatas, the vocal score of *Elijah*, and his first and last compositions. It has made the Bodleian, alongside the Staatsbibliothek in Berlin, one of the two principal centres of Mendelssohn research in the world.

Purchased, 2002. *MS. M. Deneke Mendelssohn d. 71, fol. 13r*

36 'Over the Rainbow'

Harold Arlen's song 'Over the rainbow' was sung by the 17-year-old Judy Garland in the 1939 film version of *The Wizard of Oz*, and received an Oscar for the best movie song of that year. Its instant success has endured, so that it still ranks amongst the most familiar of songs. This is a copy of the first edition, published in July 1939 by Leo Feist, New York, and the cover features leading members of the cast. It is one of about 100,000 American songs, which form just one part of the vast Harding Collection, received under the bequest of Walter N.H. Harding of Chicago in 1974. Harding's main interest was in secular song from the 17th century onwards, particularly in its more popular manifestations, and his collection included great quantities of English ballads, plays with music, song

books (both with and without the music) and music-hall songs, as well as American songs from 1800 to 1950. Other areas of interest included opera scores, French song books, jest books and travel literature, all built up in the first sixty years of the twentieth century. Harding, who was born in London in 1883 and emigrated to Chicago at the age of four, wanted to see his collection find a home in his native country, hence the bequest to the Bodleian, which he never visited. The collection was the largest ever received by the Library, and enormously strengthened its already considerable resources of British song material, as well as giving it splendid resources in other fields.

Bequeathed, 1974. *Harding Mus. Q 563*

37 Gustav Holst (1874–1934), Opening of 'The Planets' Suite

Holst composed his orchestral masterpiece *The Planets* in the years 1914–16. Its seven substantial movements are matched by an appropriately-sized orchestra, and Holst actually entitled it 'Seven pieces for large orchestra'. The composer had already begun to suffer from neuritis in his right arm, and many sections of this full score were written with the assistance of amanuenses. The opening movement, 'Mars', however, is almost entirely in the composer's hand, and, contrary to popular belief, it was entirely conceived before the outbreak of the First World War. The score (now bound in seven volumes) was a gift in 1947 from the composer's daughter, Imogen, partly in memory of the recently deceased Heather Professor, Sir Hugh Allen, and partly as a thank-you present to the Bodleian, which had taken in most of Holst's manuscripts for safekeeping during the Second World War. *The Planets*

was in fact the third manuscript of the composer to find a permanent home in the Bodleian. In the 1920s the Friends of the Bodleian began to solicit examples of major British composers' manuscripts for the Library. Bax, Delius, Ethel Smythe, and Vaughan Williams were amongst those who responded positively, while Holst presented first his opera *Savitri* in 1928, and subsequently the vocal score of *A choral fantasia* in 1931. The Library has continued to seek opportunities to extend its music collections in this way, and in particular to acquire manuscripts of composers with Oxford associations, be they whole archives, such as those of George Butterworth and Gerald Finzi, or isolated manuscripts, as for example with William Walton and Geoffrey Bush.

Presented, 1947. *MS. Mus. b. 18/1, p. 1*

I The Bringer of War — Gustav von Holst

Western manuscripts, 16th to 18th centuries 38-42

38 William Stukeley's plan of Avebury stone circle in 1722

The county of Wiltshire boasts two huge stone circles—Avebury to the north and Stonehenge to the south of Salisbury Plain. When John Aubrey came across the former on a day's hunting in 1648, he considered it to 'exceed Stonehenge as a cathedral doth a parish church'. Yet Stonehenge is by far the better known to this day. This is no doubt due to its striking setting and its being nearly complete. Avebury, though much larger, is obscured by the village which developed among the stones and had already suffered much damage by 1719, when Stukeley first visited it. Stukeley was outraged by the breaking up of the stones for building material. Unable to stop the destruction, he determined to preserve a detailed record of what survived.

Stukeley's careful measurements and detailed drawings were the only evidence of the layout of the Avebury stones as they existed in the early 18th century until Alexander Keiller undertook major excavations in the 1930s. The engraving of the plan shown here, published in 1743, distinguishes between stones standing and fallen, 'the place of a stone taken away' and 'a cavity visible where a stone stood'. It is on his work at Stonehenge and Avebury that Stukeley's reputation as the father of British field archaeology rests. His first drafts of an account of the two stone circles were designed to be part of a 'History of the Temples of the Ancient Celts', based on his study of henge monuments and circles throughout Britain. By the time his accounts were published—*Stonehenge* in 1741 and *Abury* in 1743—his objective record and comments had been lost in a mass of speculation about the religious beliefs and practices of the Druids.

The bulk of the Stukeley manuscripts now in the Bodleian were acquired over a period of thirty years. Their acquisition demonstrates the way in which judicious purchases and generous gifts can bring back together an important collection dispersed at auction. One of Stukeley's daughters married Richard Fleming, Stukeley's solicitor and executor. Through their daughter, the bulk of Stukeley's manuscripts passed to the St. John family of Dinmore Court in Herefordshire; though Richard Gough acquired several volumes of drawings and manuscripts by Stukeley, which were bequeathed, with the rest of his topographical collections, to the Bodleian in 1809. The Dinmore Court collection was sold at Sotheby's in 1924, when the Library bought twenty-five manuscripts, and in 1932, when it bought five. Three donors presented a further thirteen between 1924 and 1943, while another fifty-two were bought at various times between 1924 and 1973, as they reappeared on the market. Alexander Keiller was also collecting Stukeley manuscripts from 1924 and most generously gave his great collection, for the most part handsomely bound in red morocco, in 1955.

The Bodleian's holdings of antiquarian manuscripts, ranging in date from the *Itinerary* of John Leland, antiquary to King Henry VIII, to the 20th century, and covering the majority of English counties, are one of its many strengths. They complement the extensive collections of published antiquarian and topographical works, the foundation of which was laid with the bequest of Richard Gough.

Presented, 1955. *MS. Eng. misc. b. 65, fol. 19*

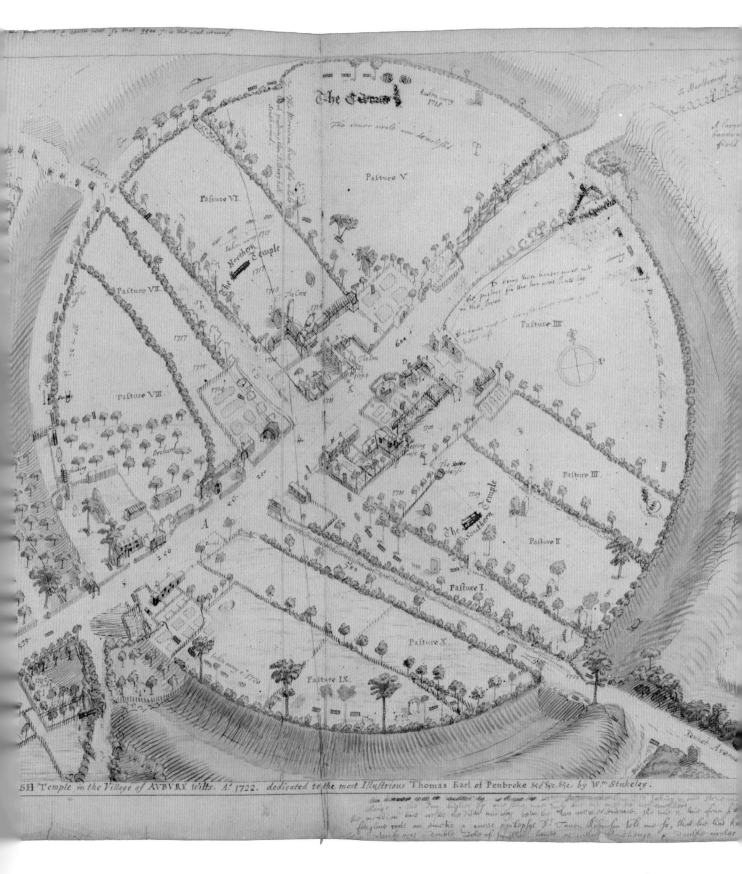

SH. Temple in the Village of AVBVRY Wilts. A.º 1722. dedicated to the most Illustrious Thomas Earl of Penbroke &c &c &c. by W.m Stukeley.

39 Notes of Charles II and Lord Chancellor Clarendon

The papers of Edward Hyde, 1st Earl of Clarendon (1609–74), which came to the Library in a series of donations between 1759 and 1888, are a major source for the study of English history in the middle of the 17th century. They provide ample evidence of Hyde's influence as the champion of the royal prerogative in the last years of Charles I's reign, as trusted adviser to Charles II in exile, as negotiator of the Restoration in 1660 and finally as Lord Chancellor from 1660 until his impeachment in 1667. Two volumes are particularly interesting in the evidence they provide about the views and characters of the King and his Chancellor and of the relationship between them. They contain about ninety notes which passed between Charles II and Clarendon during meetings of the Privy Council, when private conversations, even for the King, were not allowed. Reading these informal jottings, one has the impression of eavesdropping on the two most powerful men in the kingdom three hundred and forty years ago.

Many of the notes refer to matters of state–negotiations with France and Portugal, appointments to offices, the treatment of petitioners, both Charles I's supporters and opponents. They are often very revealing of the characters of both men and of their attitude to their contemporaries. The most famous exchange, illustrated here, nicely reveals the sense of humour of 'the Merry Monarch'. The King makes arrangements to escape from London for a couple of nights, travelling light with only his night bag. Clarendon remonstrates that he cannot go without '40 or 50 horse', which prompts the royal punchline 'I count that parte of my night bag'.

The Clarendon papers were the last of four magnificent manuscript collections which, arriving in the middle years of the 18th century, put the Bodleian at the forefront of centres for the study of 17th-century British history. First were the manuscripts of Thomas Tanner, Bishop of St. Asaph (1674–1735), equally important (in the papers of Archbishop Sancroft) for studies of the Anglican Church in the last years of the century and (in the papers of Speaker Lenthall) for the period from Charles I's personal rule to 1659. These were swiftly followed by the papers of James, 1st Duke of Ormonde as Lord Lieutenant of Ireland in the 1640s and after the Restoration—the gift of the historian Thomas Carte. The third benefaction was the collection of Richard Rawlinson (1690–1755), antiquarian and bishop in the nonjuring Church of England, who had rescued vast quantities of official papers of the previous century, among them those of John Thurloe, Secretary of State during the Protectorate and of Samuel Pepys at the Admiralty, with many relating to Monmouth's Rebellion and to the reigns of both Charles II and James II. These 18th-century acquisitions have continued to this day to attract to the Library further collections and a mass of individual volumes of 17th-century state papers.

Presented, 1759. *MS. Clarendon 100, fol. 54*

28   54

I would willingly make a visite to my sister at
tunbridge for a night, or two at farthest, when do
you thinke I can ~~you~~ best spare that time?

I know no reason why you may not for such
a tyme, (2. nights) go the next weeke,
about Wensday, or Thursday, and where we tyme
enough for the adiournement: which you out
to be the weeke followinge.

I suppose you will goe with a light
Trayne.

I intend to take nothing but my night bag.

yet, you will not go without 40. or 50.
horse.

I counte that parte of my night bag.

40 Virginia versus Maryland in 1635

Rivalries between different groups of settlers in North America are well-illustrated in this document, a summary of the complaints of the Planters of Virginia against their own Governor, Sir John Harvey, and a group of newly-arrived emigrants from England. The newcomers had landed at Point Comfort on 27 February 1634, having survived a four-month voyage in two ships optimistically named the *Ark of Avalon* and the *Dove*. They were led by Leonard Calvert, the younger brother of Lord Baltimore, who had been granted land north of the Potomac to found the new colony of Maryland.

The Virginians claimed that, despite their friendly assistance, in the shape of pilots, interpreters, and boats, Lord Baltimore's people, encouraged by Harvey, had offered violence to the plaintiffs who were peacefully going about their trading. The dispute was not settled quickly, as one side after the other resorted to law, then to force. Religious differences exacerbated territorial claims, for Calvert and the 1634 arrivals were all Roman Catholics, while the earlier settlers were predominantly Puritans. It was only in 1646 that Calvert was finally established as Governor of Maryland.

This document survives in one of the bundles of papers of Sir John Bankes, who was Attorney-General to King Charles I from 1634 to 1640. Bankes annotated several in the bundle and no doubt advised the King on the claims and counter-claims which were sent to London for resolution. The Bankes papers, some 2300 documents in all, are an important source for the history of King Charles's reign. They were completely unknown to historians until the 1950s—unlike the majority of the Bodleian's rich collections of 17th-century state papers which came into the Library in the middle years of the 18th century.

Sir John remained loyal to the King when the Civil War broke out and attended the court at Oxford. He died in 1644 and is buried in Christ Church Cathedral. As a Royalist his estate was forfeit. His castle at Corfe was slighted. His papers disappeared for 300 years. They were discovered in 1949 in the estate office (a converted laundry) of Lydney Park in Gloucestershire. Their owner, Lord Bledisloe, an honorary DCL of the University and honorary Fellow of University College, sold them for a very modest sum to the Bodleian.

Purchased, 1959. *MS. Bankes 8, fol. 43r*

A Breviat of the Declaration
of the Planters in Virginia
Dated the 30.th of July, 1635

The Lo: Baltimore's Ship the Arke arrived at Point
Fol. 1. A. Comfort in Virginia ffebr: 1633 who brought letters from
his Ma.tie that all good correspondence should be held betwixt
them and assistance given them w.ch was accordingly performed
by furnishing them w.th Pilots, Interpreters, Boate and
Pinnace, and from thence they sailed into Patomeke River,
the uttermost part of their Limitts.

At their first arrivall there, before they seated themselves,
Fol. 1. A. and B. they offered violence to our Planters of Virginia then trading
in that River, wholly ignorant of the new Grant by seizing
of their persons and Vessells, even on the South side of
Patomeke river, w.ch is out of their Limitts, and interdicted
them trade.

This Interdiction of trade Captaine Clayborne and
Fol. 1. B. his men refusing to obey, Josiah Stratton a Planter of
Virginia was employed by the Governour of Maryland to
arrest their persons Vessells and Goods, w.ch he attempted by
shooting at them, and fayling of his purpose, another way is
sought out to call even his life and estate into question.

S.r John Harvey and Captaine Purfoy took the deposition
Fol. 1. B. of Henry Fleete in Maryland May 1634, wherein he certifies
Clayborne for practising w.th the Indians to destroy those of
Maryland w.ch deposition being there only knowne and done
was by the Governour of Maryland by the last Ship that
went for England certifyed to his Ma.tie, that the
accusation might appeare w.thout any answere.

41   A Royal New Year's gift of 1545

This remarkable example of the writing and translating skills of Queen Elizabeth I when she was just 11 years old came to the Library in 1729, in a collection of otherwise unremarkable manuscripts given by the widow of Francis Cherry. Cherry was a man of means, a resident of Shottesbrooke in Berkshire, who had matriculated at St. Edmund Hall in 1682, but had never taken a degree. He was the generous benefactor of many scholars, among them the Oxford antiquary Thomas Hearne, whose school and university education he paid for. Unable to accept the legitimacy of the Revolution in 1688, he became a nonjuror and spent much of his fortune assisting those clergy who were deprived of their livings for refusing to take the oath of allegiance to William and Mary. No mean scholar, Cherry is reckoned also to have been a bold rider, whom King William was in the habit of following closely when out stag hunting. An intriguing anecdote survives of Cherry leaping down a steep and dangerous bank into the River Thames in the hopes that 'the usurper' would follow him to his death; but the King wisely turned away his horse at the last minute.

There is some doubt about the route by which the Cherry manuscripts reached the Bodleian. The Benefactors' Register records them as a bequest, but Hearne noted in his diary that Cherry had given them to him. They finally arrived, through the good offices of Cherry's daughter Anne, who added a portrait of her father to her mother's gift of the manuscripts.

This manuscript is one of the Library's great royal treasures. It contains Elizabeth's own translation, carefully written in her fine italic hand, of a French devotional poem—'Le miroir de l'âme péchéresse' by Margaret of Angoulême, sister of the French King and wife of the King of Navarre. The young princess dedicated it to her step-mother, Catherine Parr, inviting her to 'rubbe out, polishe and mende … the wordes', and asking her not to let anyone else see it, until it had been corrected 'lesse my faultes be knowne of many'. Catherine is known to have taken a kindly interest in the education of her two young step-children; so it is reasonable to conjecture that she introduced Princess Elizabeth to Margaret of Angoulême's religious verse. When in 1548 the translation was published with a long dedication to Elizabeth by the ultra-Protestant John Bale, the wording had indeed been polished, but whether by the Queen or by Bale it is impossible to say. Tradition has it that Elizabeth also embroidered the binding, with silver and gold stitches on a blue silk ground, the queen's initials in the centre of each cover and heart's-ease in each corner.

Presented, 1729.   *MS. Cherry 36, fol. 2r and binding*

TO OVR MOST ENNOBLE AND
vertuous quene KATHERIN, Eliza
beth, her humble daughter wisheth;
perpetuall felicitie and euerlasting ioye

NOT ONELY knowing the affec
tuous wille and feruent zeale the
wich your highnes hath towardes
all godly lerning as also my ductie
towardes you (most gracious and
                    prince:
souueraine) but knowing also that
pufilanimite and yeliece are most
repugnante vnto a reasonable crea
ture and that (as the philosopher
fayeth) euen as an instrument of yron

42 Water-colour drawing of a 'design for the state bed' for William Beckford at Fonthill, by Sir John Soane, 1788

William Beckford (1760–1844) was the author of the oriental travel novel *Vathek* (1784), *Dreams, waking thoughts, and incidents* (1783, but suppressed), and other works. In 1788 he was living at Fonthill Abbey, the mansion inherited from his father (William Beckford, Lord Mayor of London in 1762 and 1769) in 1770. Beckford spent large amounts of money (mainly income from estates in the West Indies) in extending, decorating, and furnishing Fonthill, where he gathered large collections of paintings, furniture, works of art, and books. In 1822 he sold Fonthill (whose main tower collapsed soon afterwards), and moved to Lansdown Tower, Bath, where he remained for the rest of his life. Large parts of Beckford's collection were sold during his lifetime, but his library was inherited by his daughter Susan, Duchess of Hamilton, and was sold at Sotheby's in the 1880s (the Hamilton Palace sales). The Beckford papers remained in the possession of the Hamiltons until 1977, when they were sold at Sotheby's, and bought by B.H. Blackwell Ltd. In July 1984 Blackwells generously gave the papers to the Bodleian 'in memory of the late Sir Basil Blackwell, his father Benjamin, and his elder son Richard, the first three chairmen of the firm'.

The papers were extensively used by Boyd Alexander for his books on Beckford, before they came to the Bodleian, and continue to be consulted regularly by Beckford scholars. They include a long series of letters from Beckford, in Italian, to his amanuensis Gregorio Franchi, many letters from Franchi and others to Beckford, journals kept by Beckford, and many drafts and fair copies of literary works, as well as music, inventories of furniture, and newspaper cuttings collected by Beckford.

Beckford read widely, and very often annotated his books on the flyleaves (usually with quotations from the book, but sometimes making a comment), and many of his reading notes are preserved in the papers, mainly as transcripts. About 30 books from Beckford's library have so far been identified in the Bodleian collections.

Sir John Soane (1763–1837), the artist of this water-colour, was the architect (designer of the Bank of England) and collector, who founded the Soane Museum in London.

Presented, 1977. *MS. Beckford b. 8, fol. 1*

*Design for the State bed
at Fonthill.*

Soane Arch.t

Welbeck Street, Jan.ry 1788.

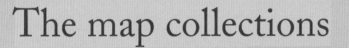

The map collections

43–45

43 The Gough Map

The Gough Map of Great Britain (also known as The Bodleian Map) is the oldest surviving road map of Great Britain, dating from around 1360. Drawn in pen, ink and coloured washes on two skins of vellum, the map's dimensions measure 115 x 56cm. It was bequeathed to the Bodleian Library by Richard Gough (1735–1809). Little is known of its provenance, other than that the map was bought by Gough at a sale in 1774 for half a crown (12½ pence). Gough noted at the time of the map's purchase that many of the place names were faded beyond recognition. The identity of the map-maker is unknown, the clues to its accurate dating based on historical changes of place name and studies of the hand used to inscribe those names onto the map.

Not only was Gough a collector of all things topographical, he also published three prominent contributions to antiquarian literature: *British topography*, *Sepulchral monuments*, and his edition of Camden's *Britannia*. Under the terms of Gough's will, he left all his manuscripts, printed books and pamphlets, maps and copperplates relating to British topography, to 'be placed in the Bodleian Library, in a building adjoining to the Picture Gallery, known by the name of the Antiquaries' Closet, erected for keeping manuscripts, printed books, and other articles relating to British topography; so that all together they may form one uniform body of English

antiquities'. A catalogue of the collection by Bulkeley Bandinel was published in 1814, a year after he became Bodley's Librarian.

The map, which is roughly at a scale of 1:1,000,000, shows east at the top, and once this is apparent, then the outline of Great Britain quickly becomes familiar. Rivers are given strategic importance, with the Severn, Thames and Humber predominant, and even the loop of the Wear at Durham readily evident. Other physical features are identified by symbols, for example a tree locates the New Forest. Particularly accurate, in terms of cartography, is the area between Hadrian's Wall and The Wash, as well as the distances between towns along the South Coast. Scotland assumes an unfamiliar shape, but the Clyde and Forth are easily identifiable, as is Edinburgh. Throughout, towns are shown in some detail, the lettering for London and York coloured gold, while other principal medieval settlements such as Bristol, Chester, Gloucester, Lincoln, Norwich, Salisbury and Winchester are lavishly illustrated. Routes between towns are marked in red on the map, with distances included in Roman numerals, also marked in red, best seen on those roads radiating out from London, and also along the Welsh coast.

Bequeathed, 1809. *MS. Gough Gen. Top. 16*

44 The Laxton Map

Mark Pierce, *A plat and description of the whole mannor & Lordship of Laxton with Laxton Moorehouse in ye county of Nottingham and also of the mannor & Lordship of Kneesall lying adiacent to ye aforesaid mannor of Laxton.* 1635.

In 1942 the 'Laxton Map' (and terrier) was bought by Library for £300 from the collection of the 6th Earl Manvers at Thoresby Park, Nottinghamshire about 10km north west of Laxton, which itself is located 15km north of Newark on Trent.

The map is all the more remarkable as its representation of a 17th-century landscape dominated by an open field system remains valid as Laxton has retained around a quarter of this field system into the 21st century. It survived as a community of tenant farmers, working the land 'in common', subject to a Court Leet.

The map was commissioned by Sir William Courten, owner of the Laxton Estate in 1635. His surveyor, Pierce, had previously produced maps in Devon, Essex, Hertfordshire, Kent, Northamptonshire and Worcestershire, thus was suitably qualified to undertake the project. The map is fully coloured and now divided into nine pieces, each measuring around 75cm x 60cm at a scale of roughly 1:3,950—16 inches to the mile.

The village of Laxton appears in the north centre of the map, neighbouring Kneesall towards the south-west. Clearly visible are the strips of land farmed on the estate, as well as pasture, woodland, individual trees, streams, roads, tracks and buildings. People and animals are also depicted, for example there are ploughing teams, and even a pair of stags locking antlers.

The Library also possesses an accompanying terrier, which describes each of the thousands of strips of land shown on the map. Every strip has a unique alpha-numeric reference, from which it is possible to identify the person farming each parcel of land, that person's status, and the acreage of each strip. All dwellings are also included, along with details of their occupants. A combination of these two items ensures that those surviving features of the landscape can still be documented almost 370 years later.

Purchased, 1942. *MS. C17:48(9)*

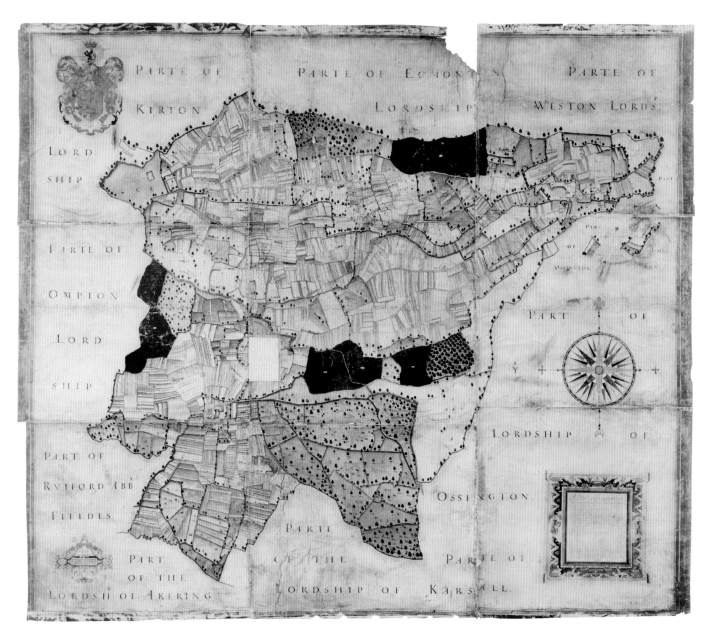

45 Henley surveyed, 1875–78

Ordnance Survey, Britain's national mapping agency, was established in 1791 and commenced publishing maps in the early nineteenth century, initially at a scale of one inch to one mile, covering the south coast of England. Ordnance Survey has been an assiduous depositor of cartographic material ever since, to such an extent that the intellectual value of legal deposit has manifested itself ever more profoundly from the 1990s onwards. Only the British Library and the Bodleian hold a virtually complete collection of Ordnance Survey maps—there is no record documenting Ordnance Survey's full publishing portfolio. Ordnance Survey lost much of its historical archive when its headquarters in Southampton fell victim to enemy action during the Second World War. A change in legislation under the aegis of the 1990 Environmental Protection Act requires property developers to undertake a thorough historical land-use audit of their proposed sites, thus environmental consultants have been drawn to access the Library's holdings of Ordnance Survey material to research landscape change across Great Britain.

This beautiful hand-coloured map is part of the First Edition 25 inches to one mile *County Series* map of Oxfordshire. Surveyed in 1875 by Lieutenant H.R.G. Georges and in 1878 by Captain G.W. Archer, both Royal Engineers, and published in 1879, this sheet features parts of the Oxfordshire parishes of Henley on Thames and Rotherfield Greys, and Berkshire's Remenham. Items of note include most of the town of Henley, as well as

the river. Individual buildings and gardens are clearly identified, while the street pattern has changed little in the intervening years. One of the principal strengths of the first edition at this scale are the numbers found all over the map (such as the 272 just to the east of Henley railway station). These figures appear in accompanying *area books*, arranged by parish, which outline the physical area of each parcel of land, and also provide a brief indication of what could be found in each parcel at the time of survey, for example stating whether fields might be 'arable' or 'pasture'. Maps at this scale covering Henley have subsequently been published in 1899, 1962, 1968 and 1992; and in 1986, 1989 and 1996 as aperture cards, though none match this 1879 sheet in terms of aesthetic beauty.

The mid-1990s saw the large scale map of Britain becoming fully digitised. As a result, maps such as the Henley sheet are no longer published, but 'printed on demand' and consequently do not fall within the terms of the 1911 Copyright Act. However, the legal deposit libraries have brokered an arrangement with Ordnance Survey whereby the libraries receive an annual snapshot of the country's most detailed mapping for the whole of Great Britain—the equivalent of 230,000 new paper maps each year, viewable on screen in the map rooms of each institution.

Legal deposit, 1879. *O.S. Counties Series, 1st ed., Oxon. sheet LIV/9*

Play
Ground

Phillis Court
On Site of
Phillis Court

B.M.115·7 BELL LANE

B.M.111·3

152ᵃ

Wharf

162ᵃ

Malthouse

St. Mary's
Hall

N E B.M.113·9
W

STREET

Malthouse

Malthouse

F.S.

B.M.115·7

Henley
Brewery
188
Grave Yard

Almshouses

St. Mary's
Church
(Rectory)

Savings Bank
B.M.119·6
H A R T STREET
B.M.119·1

Malthouse

Malthouse

Grammar
School

Rectory

Henley
Works
(Iron)

B.M.115·6

NEW STREET
P.H.

P.H.

Greys
Brewery

B.M.116·3

Southfield
House

Malthouse

FRIDAY STREET

Royal Hotel B.M.105·7

River
Terrace

Steam Saw
Mill

107ᵃ

W.B.C.

F.S.

B.M.108·9

Barge Building
Sheds

Und

R I V E R

Municipal Boundary

B.M.107·9

P.

P.H.

B.M.107·4

Red Lion Hotel

T H A M E S

T E R R A C E

Hotel

Boat House

Boat House

Und

B.M.120·4

B.M.108·9

Henley on Thames

C.R.

Hen

l

e

TOWING PATH

87

89
F.S.

Cricket Ground
90

93

HENLEY
ON
THAMES

94

Carpenters Arms
(P.H.)

110

Angel
(P.H.)
B.M.109·9

Bird
Place

108

109

Two Brewers
(P.H.)
B.M.108

96

97

93ᵃ

98

95

G.P.

123

120

111

Boat House
Thamesfield

The oriental collections

46-66

46 A manuscript of 'Alexander's Wall', a poem in Chagatay by Ali Șir Nevai, copied in 1485

'Alexander's Wall' is one of the five poems that go to make up Ali Șir Nevai's Quintet. Written in the Eastern Turkic literary language known as Chagatay, the Quintet is modelled on a similar composition of the same name by the celebrated 12th-century Persian poet Nizami. Nevai (1441–1501) was born in Herat and rose to become chief minister to the sultan Husayn Bayqara. He played an important role as a statesman and patron of the arts and is considered the greatest exponent of Chagatay literature. Nevai was also an accomplished poet in the Persian language.

The manuscript is one of a set of four in the Library. The fifth manuscript, completing the Quintet, is now in the John Rylands Library in Manchester. The four Bodleian manuscripts between them contain eleven miniatures, all contemporary with the date of copying; some folios containing miniatures appear to have been removed. This manuscript contains four miniatures and is open at the depiction of Iskandar (Alexander) enthroned. One of the other miniatures in the manuscript, 'Mystics discoursing in a garden', has been attributed to Bihzad, the most famous of Persian artists. If not by the master himself it is certainly very close to his style. The binding is of painted lacquer with floral designs and has been assigned to the 18th century.

The Elliott collection, to which this manuscript belongs, consists of over 400 volumes. It was received by the Library as a gift in 1859. Its owner, John Bardoe Elliott of the Bengal Civil Service, had acquired, in the course of building his collection of Persian manuscripts and printed books, many of the manuscripts of Sir Gore Ouseley. Sir Gore Ouseley went to India as a young man in 1787 and spent his early years in Lucknow, where he began collecting manuscripts for himself and his elder brother William. He had an eye for illustrated and illuminated manuscripts and was able to enhance his collection when, from 1810 to 1814, accompanied by his brother, he undertook a diplomatic mission to the Court of Persia. Elliott had originally bequeathed his collection to the British Museum but late in his life he was persuaded by one Mr. Fitz-Edward Hall that it would be more fitting if his collection came to the Bodleian Library to join the other Ouseley manuscripts—Sir William's collection had already been bought in 1843.

Presented, 1859. *MS. Elliott 339, binding*

47 Yusuf u Zulaykha by the Persian poet Jami—a manuscript dated 1569

A painted Persian binding with envelope flap, probably of the second half of the 16th century. The outside covers and flap are of dark green lacquer painted in gold and various colours with depictions of animals, birds, trees, flowers and clouds. The doublures (insides of the covers) are of leather with medallions and corner pieces of cut-out work in gold on blue and green. The binding is probably contemporary with the manuscript, which is dated September–October 1569.

The manuscript itself contains the poem entitled *Yusuf u Zulaykha*, a legendary life of Joseph and the pharaoh Potiphar's wife, by the 15th-century Persian poet Jami (1414–92). It contains a fine double illuminated title-page and six miniatures in the Qazvin style (Qazvin was the capital of the Safavid dynasty from 1548 to 1598). The manuscript testifies both to John Greaves's discriminating taste in manuscripts and his interest in Persian language and literature.

Purchased, 1678. *MS. Greaves 1, binding*

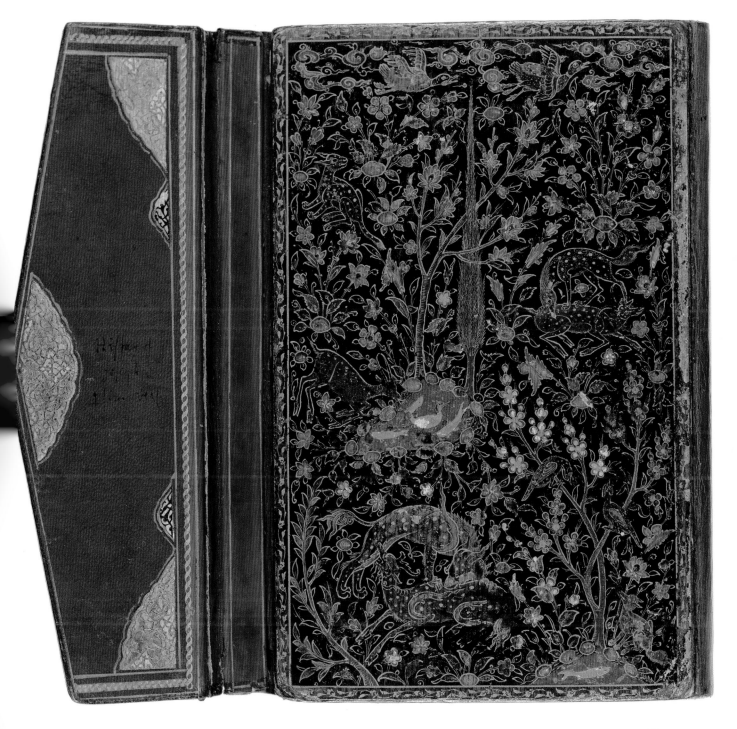

48 A Persian manuscript of the Ruba'iyat of 'Umar Khayyam, copied in Shiraz in 1460

'Umar Khayyam's dates are unsure but 1048 is accepted as a possible date of birth, and his date of death is commonly placed in 1123. He was a native of the important city of Nishapur in North East Persia. In the Islamic world he is known traditionally more as an astronomer and mathematician than as a poet. He made important contributions to algebra and wrote also on numbers and geometry. In addition he was instrumental in the work of reforming the Persian solar calendar, a task which was begun in 1074. The celebrity of 'Umar Khayyam's 'ruba'iyat' or quatrains stems from the publication of Edward Fitzgerald's paraphrase, the first version of which was published by Quaritch in 1859. Although few copies of the first version were sold the Rubaiyat went on to enjoy spectacular success.

This Ouseley manuscript was discovered in the Bodleian Library in 1856 by E.B. Cowell, who had taught Edward Fitzgerald Persian at Cambridge. The manuscript contains 158 quatrains explicitly attributed to 'Umar Khayyam (the question of the authenticity of the quatrains ascribed to him in the various extant manuscripts is a major issue). It is written in an elegant nasta'liq hand. Fitzgerald did not actually use the Ouseley manuscript direct but a copy prepared from it by Cowell. He also made use of a later Indian copy containing a larger number of quatrains. Fitzgerald's Rubaiyat undoubtedly played a major part in introducing Persian poetical themes to the western reading public for the first time.

The orientalist and collector Sir William Ouseley had accompanied his brother Sir Gore on an embassy to Persia during the years 1810–1814 and was able to enhance the collection of several hundred Persian manuscripts he had already been able to assemble in London. The Bodleian purchased Sir William's collection in 1843, a year after his death.

Purchased, 1843. *MS. Ouseley 140, fols. 41v–42r*

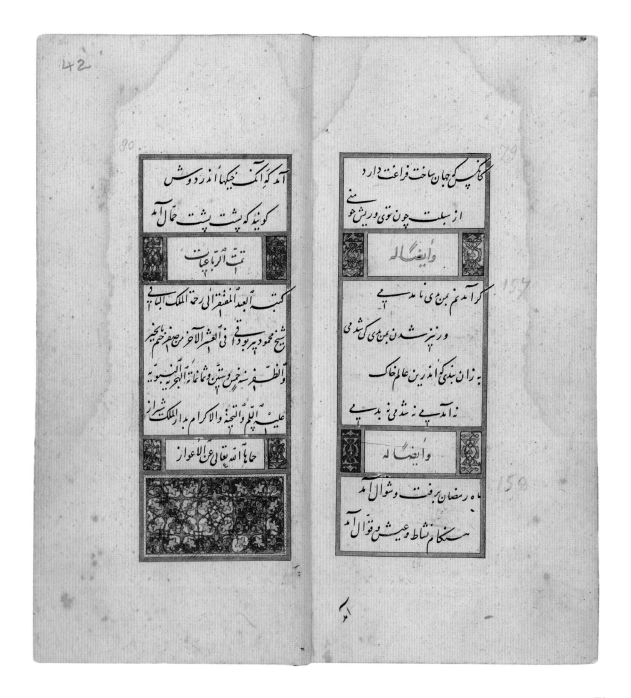

49 An Armenian manuscript of the Four Gospels, copied in Julfa in 1596

The manuscript contains eleven miniatures illustrating events from the life of Christ and the four evangelists. The verso of the first leaf depicts the Last Judgement, with Christ enthroned on the four symbolic beasts. The Virgin and John the Baptist stand at his sides. The scales of justice hang from the lower frame, the left tray loaded with the fruits of good works resting on the back of a demon. An angel, standing on the left, witnesses the weighing of good and evil deeds. The facing miniature is a nativity scene, inscribed 'The birth of Christ in Bethlehem and the Shepherds'. The artist is the well-known Hakob Jughayetsi (*c.*1550–1613) of Jugha, whose signature appears in an inscription below the portrait of St. Matthew. The manuscript was copied by the scribe Anania vardapet Shabetsi 'at the door of the church of Saint Step'annos in the city of Jugha'. It was bought by the Library at auction in July 1972.

The Bodleian's first Armenian manuscript acquisitions date back to the benefactions of Archbishop Laud during the years 1635 to 1640. Further items were acquired when the Library purchased Thomas Marshall and Edward Pococke's collections of Oriental manuscripts, in 1685 and 1693 respectively. Several more Armenian manuscripts came with Archbishop Marsh's bequest of 1713. Since the end of the 19th century more than a hundred further manuscripts have been purchased by, or given to, the Library.

One of Laud's gifts was an early Armenian printed book, a copy of the Venice Psalter of 1587. The Pococke collection also contained an early printed item, the only known copy of a Psalter which, according to the colophon, was printed at Julfa, Isfahan, in 1638. Other early printed books are to be found scattered among the Selden, Marshall and Douce collections. A number of printed books in Armenian were presented to the Library in 1707 by Thomas Vanandets'i, Archbishop of the Holy Cross in Gogthan, Greater Armenia, on his visit to Oxford. The books he presented were works printed at his own press in Amsterdam.

Purchased, 1972. *MS. Arm. d.25, fols. 1v–2r*

50 Drawings of a machine for raising water from a pool or well, from an Arabic manuscript of The Book of Knowledge of Ingenious Mechanical Devices, copied in Syria or Iraq in 1486

Little is known about al-Jazari, the author of this mechanical treatise. He lived in the 12th and 13th centuries and completed the composition of this work in 1204 or 1206. The name al-Jazari derives from the geographical area of 'al-Jazirah', the land between the upper reaches of the Tigris and the Euphrates. The work contains careful descriptions of the construction of various mechanical devices, illustrated with explanatory drawings. In addition to water-raising devices it deals with the construction of clocks, vessels and figures suitable for drinking sessions, pitchers and basins for handwashing and blood-letting, fountains, and locks and bolts.

The manuscript belongs to one of the Library's smaller Islamic collections. The Greaves Oriental manuscripts were purchased from the estate of Thomas Greaves in 1678 but they had formerly belonged to Thomas's brother John, who died in 1652. Thomas served as Deputy Professor of Arabic at Oxford during

Edward Pococke's three-year stay in Constantinople. His brother John was Professor of Geometry at Gresham College and later, between 1643 and 1648, was Savilian Professor of Astronomy at Oxford. Besides mathematics and astronomy he developed an interest in Near Eastern languages. In 1637 he set off with his friend Pococke for Constantinople. An important reason for his journey was the collection of manuscripts, especially scientific manuscripts in Arabic and Persian, both for himself and for Archbishop Laud. The other purpose was to carry out astronomical observations, which he did on Rhodes and in Alexandria. Whilst in Egypt he visited and measured the pyramids at Saqqara. The results were published in his book *Pyramidographia*, published in 1646. Greaves published various Arabic and Persian astronomical and scientific works and, in addition, a grammar of the Persian language.

Purchased, 1678. *MS. Greaves 27, fols. 99v–100r*

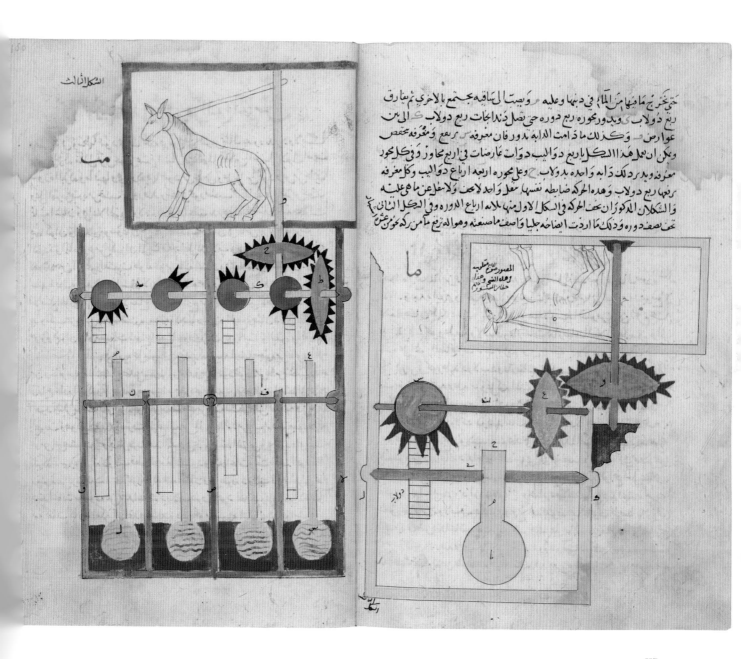

51   The Eastern Mediterranean coast with part of the island of Cyprus and the Syrian hinterland in The book of Roger, copied in Cairo in 1553

The book of Roger is a geographical compendium consisting of a preface followed by a description of the world divided according to the seven traditional Greek climes (horizontal divisions parallel to the equator). The seven climes are further divided into ten sections, making a total of seventy divisions. Each of the seventy divisions of text has a corresponding sectional map in the book. This map is labelled 'part 5 of the third clime'. Al-Idrisi's is the first Islamic geographical work to be divided in this way. Six of the extant manuscripts of al-Idrisi's work, including the two Bodleian copies, have, in addition to the sectional maps, a circular world map at the front. Although this is frequently known as the 'al-Idrisi world map' it is not actually referred to by al-Idrisi in the text of his work and its presence remains somewhat enigmatic.

Details of the life of the author are sketchy. According to some he was born in Ceuta, Morocco, in 1100 and was educated in Cordoba. He began his travels at the age of 16, visiting Asia Minor, the southern coast of France, England, Spain, and North Africa. In about 1138 he was invited by Roger II (1097–1154), the Norman king of Sicily, to his court in Palermo. In collaboration with others at the court, al-Idrisi completed his geographical compendium and, in addition, a world map engraved on silver, which is no longer extant. The geography was

completed in January 1154 and is an exhaustive account of the known world's physical, cultural and political features. After the death of Roger II, al-Idrisi stayed on at the court of his son and successor William I. According to some authorities, towards the end of his life he returned to North Africa, where he died in 1165.

This manuscript is one of over 400 mainly Arabic and Hebrew manuscripts that comprise the magnificent collection of Edward Pococke. The collection was bought by the Library from his widow in 1692, a year after his death. Pococke was the foremost Arabist of his time and was the first incumbent of the Laudian chair of Arabic set up at Oxford by Archbishop Laud. He gave his inaugural lecture in August 1636. (Pococke also held the Regius Professorship of Hebrew from 1648.) He had spent the years 1630 to 1635 as chaplain to the merchants of the Levant Company in Aleppo and from 1637 he spent three years in Constantinople. Throughout his stays in the Near East he pursued his study of the Arabic language and collected manuscripts both for himself and for Archbishop Laud. He continued to collect manuscripts, through agents, after his return from Constantinople. It is not known where or how Pococke acquired his manuscript of al-Idrisi.

Purchased, 1692. *MS. Pococke 375, fols. 123v–124r*

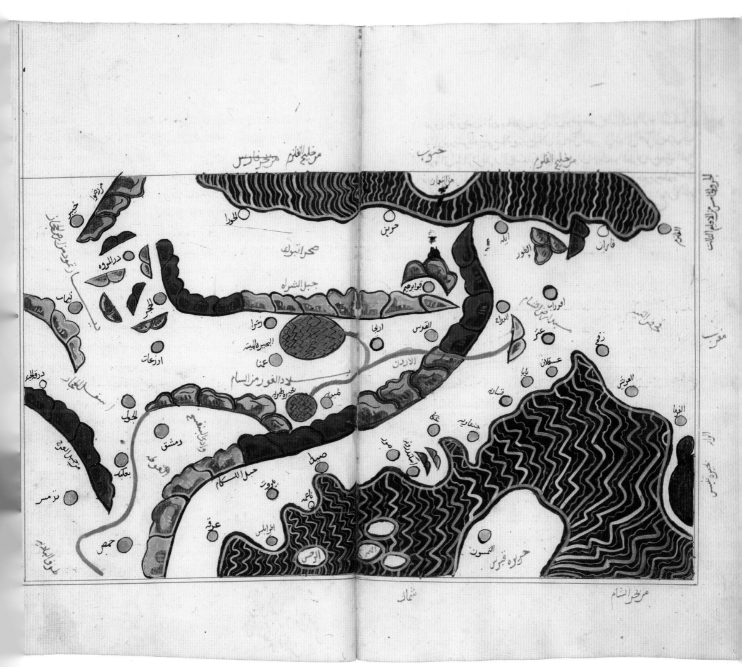

52 An early Yiddish book of customs

As well as Hebrew manuscripts (item 53) the Oppenheimer collection contains a rich assembly of early printed books. As, unusually, the collector was interested in acquiring items which were commonly discarded, the Bodleian found itself in possession of the world's finest collection of early printed books in Yiddish. In writing, Yiddish had an inferior status to Hebrew, and was chiefly used to address women, children, and males ignorant of Hebrew; significantly, the first book printed in Yiddish (Cracow, 1534) is a translation of difficult phrases in biblical Hebrew. For the same reason, early books in Yiddish were badly printed and ephemeral, and so have survived (if at all) in very few copies. In some cases the Bodleian example is unique. One of the more popular items in this genre were Books of Customs (Minhogim), often illustrated, as in this example. The woodcut shows the baking of Matsot (Matses), a common motif. Other genres in the collection are dirges after plagues and conflagrations and 'beautiful poems' of celebration. Of more recent date, of course, than the material in the Oppenheimer collection, the Bodleian also possesses a rich library of socialist literature written in the 'proletarian' language (Yiddish) as opposed to the 'bourgeois and clerical' language (Hebrew).

Purchased, 1829. *Opp. 4° 1006, fol. 21r*

נוך דער פינפֿט שעה׳ ∶ זול ער זן כל חמירא׳ ∶ וויא אובֿן שטיט רטן ער
דארף עט אף ורייטג ניט בור שטורין רט וויל ער נוך שבת סעודות
שילעטן ∶ אף שבת לו אורטן דערף אן ניט שפֿעטהר עטן אן ויר שעות
אויך רטן טג ∶

דיא בכורים ואלטן אף ערב פסח ∶ רט וויל זיא בֿטירטט זיין ווארן
די יורן בכורים אין מצרים אוב׳ זיין ניט אוף קומן רט׳ ∶ גֿלייכן אך
מייניר דערמיין בֿכור מיז נואיירט לו זיינר אוטר אוז אך ואטטן ∶ אוז׳ ער
הייטט בֿכור שוטה ∶ רטן ערטואו אף ערב פסח ואטטן ∶ אוז׳ יַדִשְּׁף ניט
פֿיְשָׁנֵיְ ∶ אז מיין אנדר דער לו זיינים וטיר בֿכור מין ∶ (עֶרֶבֿ פֶּסַח אוף שבת
ואטטן זיא אף דורטטאג דר בֿור)

מן דארך אף ערב פסח נוך מיטג קין מלאכה טון ∶ אוז מין ניט ווי
וויניגרא∶ חול המועד גירעלבֿנט ∶ מן מג זיך אבֿיר וואל בֿארן ∶

מן דארך ווירך חמץ נוך מצה עטן אף ערב פסח נוך מיטג ∶ מן זול
אך גרינן שפֿיין עטן דאז דאז מורגנט ∶ רא∶ מן רימצה לו שטיג
עטט בֿיא נלכט ∶ מן מג וואל וטיר טרינקן אבֿיר ניט ווי ∶ אוז וויניג וויין
דארך אן ניט טרינקן ∶ אבֿירויל ווין מג אן טריינקן ∶ רטן זיל ווין אלכט
לוטטיג רענומען ∶ די גמרא טוט אוז זאגן ∶ מן מג וואל אובֿט עטן וונן
טון בֿור דער חרוסת מין ∶

דיא מצות באקן

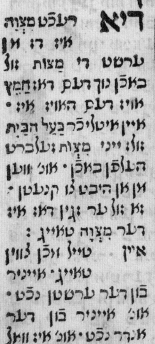

דיא רעלט מצוה
מיז דו מן
ערטט די מצות זול
באקן נוך דעם דאז חמץ
מיז דעם האוז מין ∶
מין מיטולירר בעל הבית
זול∶ יינו מצות ∶ עלזברט
הגולפֿן באקן ∶ אוז וונן
מן אן היבט לו קנעטן ∶
זא זול ער זגין דאז מין
דער מצוה טייג ∶
אין טייל וכן לווין
טייג מיינר
בֿון דער ערטן נלט ∶
אוז מיינר בֿון דער
אנדר נלט ∶ אוז מיז ואל

53   A Hebrew Prayer Book written in Germany in 1471

In 1829 the Bodleian Library bought the Oppenheimer Library, the most important and magnificent Hebraica collection ever accumulated, at a price later described as 'the best bargain in the history of bookselling'. Rabbi David ben Abraham Oppenheimer (1664–1736) was the Chief Rabbi of Prague, and devoted more than half a century to building up his library. At his death, however, the collection was the subject of litigation, and was held in storage in 28 crates in a Hamburg warehouse. As this made access to the collection virtually impossible, it was a matter of deep concern to contemporary scholars, particularly as during his lifetime Oppenheimer had been most generous with access to his manuscripts, even subsidising young scholars to publish them. However,

no-one could be found who was willing to purchase the collection for donation to a university library in Germany. In this context, the Bodleian decided to purchase the entire collection, comprising about 4350 printed books and 780 manuscripts. This acquisition nearly doubled the number of Hebrew manuscripts in the Library, and provided an in-depth coverage of the subjects known at the time. This example was written in Germany in 1471, and contains common prayers and the Ethics of the Fathers (Pirke Avot). This opening shows the beginning of chapter 4 of Pirke Avot, 'Ben Zoma omer, eizehu haham?' (Ben Zoma said, 'Who is wise?').

Purchased, 1829. *MS. Oppenheimer 776, fol. 56v–57r*

טוב וזה ה מפין שתול על פלֶגֵי מים ועֵל יבֵל ישולח
טרסיץ וליו יליֹ/הٍ כٍי יבוֹחום זהיה עליהו רעֵנן מטו
מטעת ביטרת ליו ידוֹגَليו יֵרّט מעשٍתוٍت פרי
ליעٍבֵזٍרه הٍסֵמֵזٍ יֹֹטٍ דٍינَן وفٍיٍتֹחٍי מٍרٍה והٍ/הٍם גֵֹٍ
הٍלٍ/הֹתٍתֹֹٍפֹוٍתٍ וֹֹٍבֹٍٍטٍٍרֹֹֹֹٍת פٍٍרֹٍפٍٍريٍٍٍٍتٍ לٍהٍكֹٍٍ/وֹֹٍה

כٍٍוٍٍזٍٍمٍٍنٍٍ

זٍٍٍٍٍٍٍ עٍٍٍٍٍٍٍ יٍٍٍٍٍٍٍ ...

54   A miniature copy of the Four Gospels in Syriac

Edward Pococke (1604–1691) was one of the many distinguished alumni of Oxford University whose collections were acquired for the Bodleian Library after their deaths. Archbishop Laud, himself an assiduous collector, made him his first Professor of Arabic from 1636, and later he was appointed to the Regius Professorship of Hebrew. Pococke had been chaplain to the English 'Turkey Merchants' in Aleppo from 1630 to 1635. Here he studied Oriental languages, collected manuscripts, and, as was his nature, made many friends. The manuscripts are chiefly in Arabic and Hebrew with some in other languages. This is a miniature copy of the Four Gospels in Syriac. By the late 17th century, when the manuscript was written, Syriac had been replaced as the spoken language by Arabic and accordingly the contents of each gospel are also given in Arabic, as here. The ornamental pages which follow the gospels, in this instance St. Luke's, possibly display the influence of Islamic 'carpet-pages'.

Purchased, 1691. *MS. Pococke 1, fols. 125v–126r*

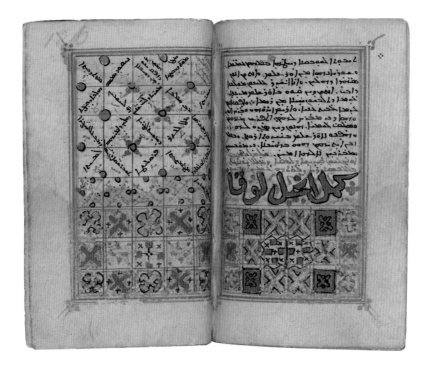

55 A grammar and dictionary of the Coptic language by Yuhanna Samannudi (13th century) in an old, undated manuscript

Coptic is the language of the liturgy of the Coptic Church in Egypt. It was formerly, down to the 10th century, the spoken language of the native population of Egypt, after which time it was gradually supplanted by Arabic. The language is a direct descendant of the ancient Egyptian language with a large admixture of Greek words and is written in a modified Greek alphabet. With the general loss of the language it became necessary to compile grammars and dictionaries in Arabic so that the Coptic scriptures remained intelligible. The dictionary section consists of a glossary of difficult words in the Coptic (Bohairic dialect) translation of the Gospels. The left-hand page shows the end of the Gospel of St. Mark, followed on the right-hand page by the beginning of the Gospel of St. Luke.

This manuscript is one of the large collection of Oriental manuscripts belonging to Robert Huntington that the Library purchased in 1692. The whole collection amounts to over 600 volumes. In 1670, Huntington took up the post of chaplain to the merchants of the Levant Company in Aleppo and he remained in the Near East for over ten years. During this time he visited Palestine, Syria, Constantinople, Egypt, and Cyprus, always looking out for manuscripts of interest to himself and to friends at home, including Edward Pococke, Thomas Marshall, and Narcissus Marsh. Huntington's concern for the Eastern Christians is evident from the large number of Christian Arabic, Coptic, and Syriac manuscripts in his collection. The collection also contains over two hundred Hebrew manuscripts.

Purchased, 1692. *MS. Huntington 590, fols. 110v–111r*

56   A Hebrew Pentateuch written in Italy in 1472

The judicious acquisition by the Bodleian Library of the Canonici manuscripts in 1817 was up to then the largest single purchase ever made by the Library. Matteo Luigi Canonici, a Venetian Jesuit, had originally intended his collection of manuscripts for the Jesuits' College at Venice. On that account neither pains nor expense were spared among his brethren, in all parts of the world, to make the collection as perfect as possible. But as the Society of Jesus remained suppressed at the time of his death in 1805 and he died intestate, the bulk of his manuscripts (in many languages) were purchased by the Bodleian for £5,444. The collection contains over 110 valuable Hebrew manuscripts, chiefly on vellum. The beginning of the biblical book of Leviticus, written in Northern Italy in 1472, has the first word of the text illuminated. For reasons unclear, Italian illumination of Hebrew manuscripts has not received the attention it merits. This folio can be contrasted with item 57 which demonstrates the same text but in a German hand of 1299.

Purchased, 1817. *MS. Can. Or. 62, fol. 87r*

מֹשֶׁה אֶת הַמְּלָאכָה ‎ ס ‎ וַיְכַס הֶעָנָן אֶת אֹהֶל
מוֹעֵד וּכְבוֹד יְהוָה מָלֵא אֶת הַמִּשְׁכָּן ׃ וְלֹא יָכֹל
מֹשֶׁה לָבוֹא אֶל אֹהֶל מוֹעֵד כִּי שָׁכַן עָלָיו הֶעָנָן וּכְבוֹד
יְהוָה מָלֵא אֶת הַמִּשְׁכָּן ׃ וּבְהֵעָלוֹת הֶעָנָן מֵעַל הַמִּשְׁכָּן יִסְעוּ
בְּנֵי יִשְׂרָאֵל בְּכֹל מַסְעֵיהֶם ׃ וְאִם לֹא יֵעָלֶה הֶעָנָן וְלֹא יִסְעוּ
עַד יוֹם הֵעָלֹתוֹ ׃ כִּי עֲנַן יְהוָה עַל הַמִּשְׁכָּן יוֹמָם וְאֵשׁ
תִּהְיֶה לַיְלָה בּוֹ לְעֵינֵי כָל בֵּית יִשְׂרָאֵל בְּכָל מַסְעֵיהֶם ׃

חסלת ספר שמות

ויקרא

וְקְרָא

אֶל מֹשֶׁה וַיְדַבֵּר יְהוָה אֵלָיו מֵאֹהֶל מוֹעֵד לֵאמֹר ׃ דַּבֵּר אֶל
בְּנֵי יִשְׂרָאֵל וְאָמַרְתָּ אֲלֵהֶם אָדָם כִּי יַקְרִיב מִכֶּם קָרְבָּן לַיהוָה
מִן הַבְּהֵמָה מִן הַבָּקָר וּמִן הַצֹּאן תַּקְרִיבוּ אֶת קָרְבַּנְכֶם ׃ אִם
עֹלָה קָרְבָּנוֹ מִן הַבָּקָר זָכָר תָּמִים יַקְרִיבֶנּוּ אֶל פֶּתַח אֹהֶל
מוֹעֵד יַקְרִיב אֹתוֹ לִרְצֹנוֹ לִפְנֵי יְהוָה ׃ וְסָמַךְ יָדוֹ עַל רֹאשׁ
הָעֹלָה וְנִרְצָה לוֹ לְכַפֵּר עָלָיו ׃ וְשָׁחַט אֶת בֶּן הַבָּקָר לִפְנֵי
יְהוָה וְהִקְרִיבוּ בְּנֵי אַהֲרֹן הַכֹּהֲנִים אֶת הַדָּם וְזָרְקוּ אֶת הַדָּם
עַל הַמִּזְבֵּחַ סָבִיב אֲשֶׁר פֶּתַח אֹהֶל מוֹעֵד ׃ וְהִפְשִׁיט אֶת
הָעֹלָה וְנִתַּח אֹתָהּ לִנְתָחֶיהָ ׃ וְנָתְנוּ בְּנֵי אַהֲרֹן הַכֹּהֵן אֵשׁ

57   A Hebrew Bible written in Germany in 1299

Dr. Benjamin Kennicott (1718–1783) devoted his life to an ambitious project to collate manuscripts of the Hebrew Bible, searching among them for variants in the original text. This labour, during which he also acquired manuscripts himself, required the assistance of scholars in foreign countries, as well as his wife. It resulted in his *Vetus Testamentum Hebraicum, cum variis lectionibus* (2 volumes, Oxford, 1776, 1780). This work resulted in the negative conclusion that the variants among the manuscripts are so slight as to be of minimal importance, and after his death his wife was left destitute. Kennicott was Radcliffe Librarian from 1767 to 1783, and in 1872 the Radcliffe Trustees deposited the Hebrew manuscripts in the Bodleian. The beginning of the Book of Leviticus, in a manuscript written in Germany in 1299, has the first word 'Va-Yikra' illuminated. The manuscript also contains the paraphrase of the Hebrew text into Aramaic, the 'Targum'. The German style can be contrasted with the more Italian style of the same word in item 56.

Presented, 1872.   *MS. Kennicott 3, fol. 100v*

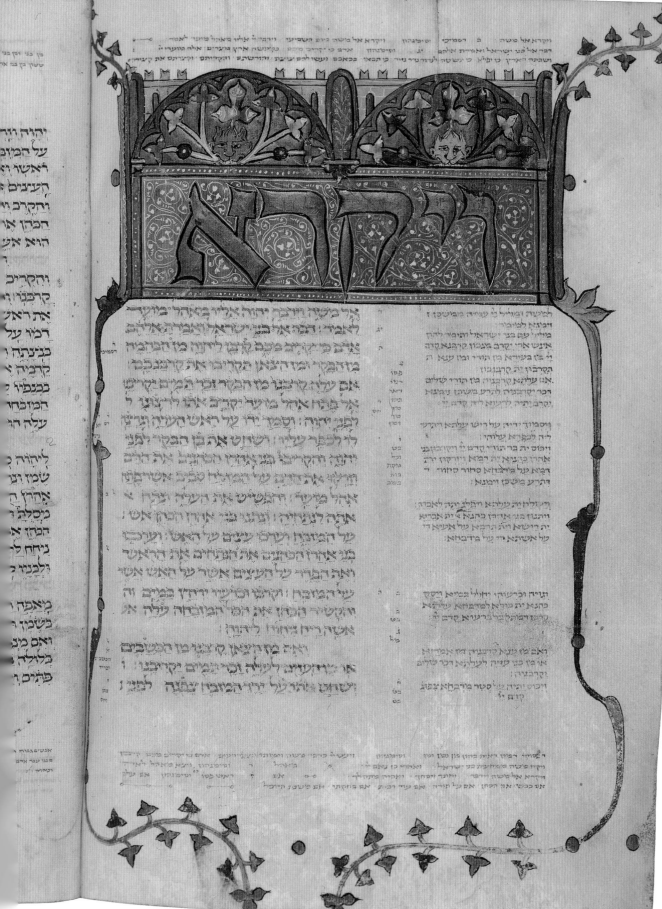

58 A firman issued by the Ottoman Sultan Murad IV in 1629

This firman (edict or order) was issued in Constantinople during the period 29 September–8 October 1629. It was sent to the Dutch ambassador with the purpose of informing him that a new consul had been appointed for the commercial activities of the Dutch merchants in Aleppo. The firman is in roll format. The Ottoman text is written in the customary divani script, a cursive form of the Arabic alphabet used for official documents. The text is highlighted by gold and red dots. The adjective divani derives from the name of the Ottoman Imperial Council (Divan-i Humayun), the script having allegedly been devised for writing its official documents and registers. At the top of the document is the calligraphic emblem (tughra) of Sultan Murad IV (reigned 1623–40). The tughra is a stylised decorative representation of the names and titles of the ruler placed as a heading on official documents.

The provenance of this firman is unknown, but it appears to be a 17th-century acquisition. It is one of over a dozen Turkish firmans in the Library and perhaps the most decorative. The first Turkish manuscript to enter the Bodleian was acquired by gift in 1602, the year of its opening. It contains a poem entitled 'The Rose and Spring' and was presented by Sir Richard Lee. Further modest numbers of Turkish items came with the Laudian and Selden donations and with the collections of Greaves, Edward Pococke, Robert Huntington, and Narcissus Marsh. When the Indian Institute Library was placed under Bodleian administration in 1927, an additional 30 Turkish manuscripts were acquired, most of them in the Eastern Turkic literary language known as Chagatay (see item 46). Other acquisitions were made by purchase at various times during the last century.

Acquired in the 17th century.   *MS. Turk. c.8 (R)*

59 The Countess of Minto's Indian Journal

This is the first volume of a nine-volume set of privately printed diaries entitled *My Indian journal* by Mary, Countess of Minto, wife of the 4th Earl of Minto, Viceroy of India from 1905 to 1910. These journals were acquired along with other papers and photographs relating to the Mintos' period in India from D.D. Evans, Day's bookshop in Thame in 1958. It is not known how these highly personal records of life in the British Raj came to end up in a Thame bookshop. The nine volumes of *My Indian journal*, bound in green morocco, are interleaved with pages of mounted photographs, postcards and newspaper clippings.

The Countess refers to the journal in her book *India, Minto and Morley, 1905–1910*: 'During our five years in India I kept a Journal, hurriedly written at odd moments of the day or night: it gives the story of our daily life, and has no merit except that it is an accurate record without which it would have been impossible to complete these pages. With some diffidence I include extracts from my Journal amongst the weighty letters which passed between the Viceroy and the Secretary of State, and have only ventured to do so in order to make the picture complete'. It is fortunate for social historians that the *Journal*, referred to so modestly by the Countess, has survived in its entirety, providing a detailed account of her heroic struggles to keep Britain alive in the midst of India. In addition to a commentary on the political issues faced by the Viceroy, who was having to deal with the consequences of the sweeping reforms implemented by his predecessor, Lord Curzon, the *Journal* provides a vivid account of the concerts, picnics, theatrical shows, hunting, and sports that characterized social life in the British Raj.

This entry is for 25 December 1905, and records her first Christmas spent at Government House, Calcutta.

On the previous page she describes the Christmas day service: 'it seemed so strange seeing the Christmas decorations composed of palms, pointsettias, bonganvlias, marigolds and nasturtians … The Christmas hymns, however, were the same, and a lady sitting in the choir kept on a mink boa throughout the service, I imagine from sentiment as it must have made her uncomfortably hot' (p. 26). The church service was followed by a large luncheon party, whose guests included Lord Kitchener and Lord Brooke: 'Our table was decorated with mistletoe, and we ate turkey, mince pies and plum pudding, otherwise sitting under the *shámiáná* with our tropical surroundings we could hardly believe that it was Christmas Day, and we thought of absent friends shivering in England in the cold raw damp, and of others in Canada with their white world sparkling in the dazzling radiance of a typical winter's day with the thermometer at zero' (pp. 26, 27).

The photographs show a traditional Indian conjuring show, which provided the after-lunch entertainment. Like many Westerners before her, the Countess seems to have been profoundly disappointed by the mango trick, where a mango seed planted by the conjuror is supposed to germinate and grow into a fruiting tree in the space of minutes. After this brief intrusion of traditional India into the festivities, the Countess of Minto's first Christmas day in Calcutta ended with the parlour game of snapdragon and an impromptu dance accompanied by the band at Government House.

Purchased, 1958. *Indian Institute 30 E 65/1*

Mary, Countess of Minto, *India, Minto and Morley, 1905–1910: compiled from the correspondence between the Viceroy and the Secretary of State, with extracts from her Indian journal*. London, Macmillan, 1934.

(27)

and we thought of absent friends shivering in England in the cold raw damp, and of others in Canada with their white world sparkling in the dazzling radiance of a typical winter's day with the thermometer at zero.

After luncheon four conjurors spread a covering on the lawn and with a wonderful flow of unintelligible language made marked rupees come out of oranges, and threaded rings on a stick which had never left the Viceroy's hands. Sundry other wonders were performed, such as cutting off each other's tongues. The mango-tree which I had always heard of as springing in five minutes from a seed to the size of Jack's bean stalk, I thought a dreadful fraud, as the seed was hidden underneath a wigwam and never grew more than three feet.

Our guests left before tea, and our evening ended in a dance and snap dragon; it is so nice having this splendid band, and it makes *impromptu* dances very easy.

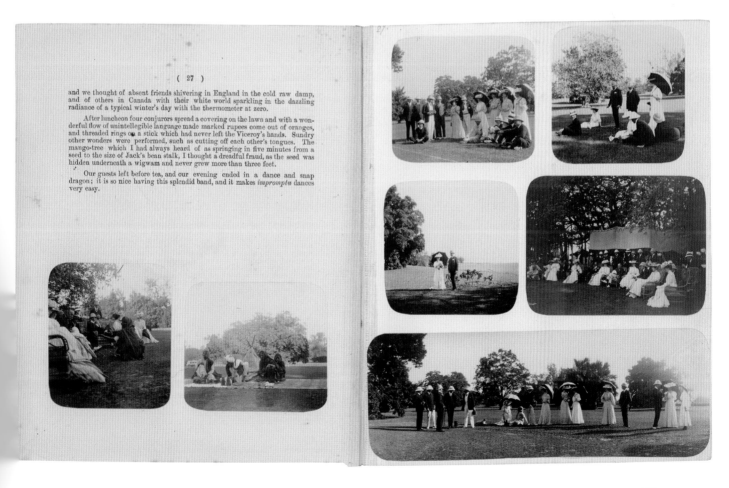

60 Two 18th-century *Bhagavadgītās*

This miniature illuminated roll containing the Sanskrit text of the *Bhagavadgītā* comes from the estate of James Fraser (d. 1754), who amassed his collection of Arabic, Persian and Sanskrit manuscripts whilst employed by the East India Company. Fraser described the 41 Sanskrit manuscripts, which were purchased at Surat and other places in India, as 'the first collection of this kind ever brought to Europe'. Whilst in India Fraser managed to learn Sanskrit, a remarkable achievement given the reluctance of Brahmins to teach their sacred language to foreigners, and had plans to work on translations into English. Unfortunately his early death at the age of 41 prevented him from becoming the first scholar ever to translate Sanskrit texts directly into English. This distinction was to go to Charles Wilkins, whose translation of the *Bhagavadgītā* was published in 1785 with financial backing from his employers, the East India Company.

The Radcliffe Trustees purchased Fraser's Oriental manuscript collection from his widow in 1758 for the sum of £500 for the Radcliffe Library. After 1811 the Library started to specialize in medicine and natural science and as its collection expanded, shelf-room became a problem. Non-scientific books and manuscripts took up valuable space needed for the expanding scientific collections, so in 1872 the Radcliffe Trustees deposited Fraser's Oriental manuscripts in the Bodleian.

This *Bhagavadgītā* is an example of an 18th-century trend in manuscript production, in which popular Hindu sacred texts were copied out on long rolls of thin, highly burnished paper in minute script, probably to be kept as amulets, conferring divine protection on the owner. The rich illuminations suggest the manuscripts were commissioned by wealthy patrons and the roll illustrated

starts with seven pictures of Hindu deities: a seated Ganesh; Brahman, also seated; two illuminations of Vishnu and Lakshmi; two paintings of Shiva and Durga; and Arjuna sitting facing Krishna.

The *Bhagavadgītā* is a text of 18 chapters found in the great Indian epic of the *Mahābhārata* but which may well have begun as a separate composition. This important Hindu text, thought to have originated between 400 BC and 200 AD, describes the rival armies of the Pandavas and Kauravas, two branches of the same family, ranged against each other on the battlefield. Arjuna, one of the Pandava brothers, is torn between his family ties to his opponents and his duty as one of the warrior caste to fight. The god Krishna advises him to engage in battle, arguing that he will only destroy the bodies of his opponents, not their souls. The *Bhagavadgītā* then goes on to offer Arjuna a spiritual path which enables him to avoid the good or bad karmic consequences of his actions and thereby escape the endless round of rebirths. Krishna advises him to take the path of *Karmayoga*: action without motivation, desire, need or expectation, without fear of failure or hope of success. In the final analysis he should dedicate all his actions to Krishna. Such disinterested action attracts no karmic consequences, either good or bad, and thus offers the possibility of spiritual progress to those still involved in affairs of the world.

Presented, 1872. *MS. Fraser Sansk. 41 a, b (R)*

G. Evison, 'The Sanskrit manuscripts of Sir William Jones in the Bodleian Library' in *Sir William Jones, 1746–1794: a commemoration.* Ed. by A. Murray. Oxford, University College, 1998.

J. Losty, *The art of the book in India.* London, British Library, 1982.

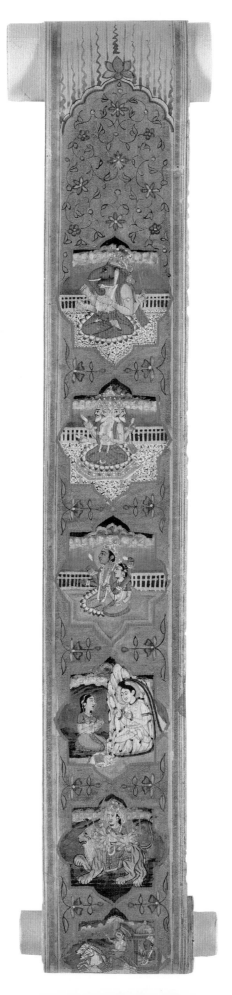

61 Rājataraṅgaṇī of Kalhaṇa: a Chronicle of the Kings of Kashmir

One of an important collection of 368 manuscripts purchased by Sir Aurel Stein (1862–1943) during his visits to Kashmir between 1888 and 1905. Although he is best known for his archaeological explorations in Central Asia and discovering the manuscripts of Dunhuang, Sir Aurel Stein also had a strong interest in the history and culture of Kashmir and from 1888 to 1889 worked on a critical edition and annotated translation of Kalhana's *Rājataraṅgaṇī.*

The *Rājataraṅgaṇī* had long held a fascination for Western scholars as the only example they could find of a historical chronicle in Sanskrit. Many of the famous names of the early days of Sanskrit scholarship had tried their hands at summaries, editions and translations, including Oxford's first Boden Professor of Sanskrit, Horace Hayman Wilson (1786–1860). Unlike his predecessors, Stein had the advantage of a number of manuscripts of the text and first-hand knowledge of the topography, archaeological remains, and local customs of Kashmir. This particular manuscript is one of the eleven in the collection that Stein used in the preparation of his critical edition and English translation of the *Rājataraṅgaṇī.* It is written in Śāradā script on old Kashmiri paper and is bound with another fragmentary *Rājataraṅgaṇī* from Stein's library.

In May 1911 Stein's collection was formally handed over to the Curators of the Indian Institute as a deposit during his lifetime and bequeathed to the library in his will. The Indian Institute had been founded by the Boden Professor of Sanskrit, Sir Monier Williams, and first opened its doors in 1884, the final phase of the building being completed in 1895. The Institute consisted of lecture rooms, a library and museum and was intended by its founder to form a focus for teaching and research on India in Oxford. The Institute's library had amassed a collection of 162 Sanskrit and Prakrit manuscripts by 1903, but Sir Aurel Stein's deposit was to treble this collection. The terms of the deposit meant that Stein kept very close control of the manuscripts during his lifetime. They had to be made available for his use whenever he required them and no scholar or student could use manuscripts of unpublished texts without Stein's express permission. When the Indian Institute Library became part of the Bodleian in 1927, its manuscripts were added to the Bodleian's growing collection of Indic primary literature, which had already been considerably augmented by the arrival of over 6,000 Indian manuscripts donated in 1909 by Maharajah Sir Chandra Shum Shere, Prime Minister of Nepal. The combined Indian Institute and Bodleian collections today form one of the largest repositories of Sanskrit manuscripts outside the Indian subcontinent.

Bequeathed to the Indian Institute, 1943. *MS. Stein Or. d. 31 (ii), fol.1*

Kalhana's Rajatarangani, or, Chronicle of the kings of Kashmir. Ed. by M.A. Stein. Bombay, Education Society's Press; Leipzig, Otto Harrassowitz, 1892.

M.A. Stein, *Kalhana's Rajatarangani: a chronicle of the kings of Kaśmir.* Westminster, Archibald Constable and Company, 1900.

62 Archbishop Laud's *Rāgamālā*

This album is one of the Bodleian Library's first South
Asian acquisitions. It is one of the 1300 manuscripts given
by Archbishop Laud between 1635 and 1641. A note on
the flyleaf records Laud's name as the donor in 1640, but
how he came by it is not known. It is of considerable
importance, not only as one of the earliest albums of
Indian art to reach Europe, but also as a rare example of
a provincial style of painting originating from outside the
Mughal capital. The style, though strongly influenced by
the Mughals, reflects the taste of a provincial collector
rather than a member of the Emperor's family. It thus
provides valuable evidence of discerning patrons outside
the very highest ranks of Mughal society.

The album itself consists of 30 paintings, of which
18 form a distinct set, part of a *Rāgamālā* cycle. These
paintings are intended to illustrate the mood and
sentiment behind the traditional forms of Indian music.
A *rāga* can be described as a combination of notes,
which form a bare skeleton out of which a song is made.
Each *rāga* tends to pivot on a particular note and these
leading notes were used as the basis for classification. In
the Northern or Hindustani system six main *rāga*s were
recognized and, since it was common to have variations
in which certain notes were omitted and the progressions
and stresses differed, the term *rāgiṇi* or subordinate *rāga*

was devised, each *rāga* then having five *rāgiṇis* associated
with it.

The *Rāgamālā* , literally 'A garland of the *rāga*s',
originated as a style of literary composition consisting
of verses in Sanskrit or Hindi personifying each of the
musical modes. The modes were arranged into families,
each *rāga* being personified as male with five wives or
rāgiṇis. These verses then came to form the theme for
albums of paintings, of which this is an example. The
painting illustrated represents the *Naṭa, Nāṭikā or Naṭ
rāgiṇī*. Although this is a 'female' melody, it symbolizes
the heroic and martial spirit, and is here depicted by a
hero fighting in battle and decapitating his enemies. It is
a *rāgiṇī* of the *Dīpika* (Fire) *rāga* and is sung in the early
hours of the night.

In addition to the 30 paintings the album contains 100
specimens of calligraphy. Some of the calligraphy is on
marbled paper; some of the borders are of papers with
gold designs, while others have been decorated with birds
and animals on a ground of soft pink.

Presented, 1640. *MS. Laud. Or. 149 (Arch. O. b.5), fol. 25r*

H. Stooke and K. Khandalavala, *The Laud Ragamala miniatures: a study in
Indian painting and music.* Oxford, Bruno Cassirer, 1953.

63 Shogun Ieyasu's *shuinjo, 1613*

The original *shuinjo* (vermilion seal document) of
1613 was issued by Shogun Tokugawa Ieyasu to grant
the English Company trade privileges in Japan. The
Bodleian's *shuinjo* is believed to be one of the two copies
given to John Saris, the commander of the eighth voyage
of the Company, the one for long presumed to be lost
in England. The exact date of its acquisition by the
library is not known, but it was included in the List of
the Bodleian manuscripts (*Library Records e.337*), which
was compiled probably in 1680. Dated the 28th day of
the 8th month, the 18th year of the Keicho (12 October
1613), the document, bearing Ieyasu's seal in vermilion
colour on top left, was issued to the captain of an English
ship, to whom it grants privileges for trade in Japan and
concomitant terms including jurisdiction rights in seven
articles.

The Bodleian's historical collections in Japanese are
not large. Nevertheless, the library has inherited some
unique treasures since its early days. The earliest known
were three volumes of *Saga-bon* (Saga Press edition)
acquired in 1629, followed by *Kirishitan-ban* (Jesuit
Press edition) and Shogun Ieyasu's *shuinjo*. However, the
Bodleian has a rich collection of pre- and early-modern
European language books dealing with Japan. This
includes examples of the published correspondence of the
Jesuit fathers, accounts of early travels to Japan in various
published records of European voyages overseas, material
relating to the East India Companies of England and
Holland, and works of European explorers of the 18th
and 19th centuries. The material colourfully illustrates
Europe's contacts with Japan from the 16th to the mid-
19th century.

Despite the early start, the Japanese language
collection was but sparsely represented in the Library in
the following centuries. A few sporadic acquisitions were
made from the library of Orientalists and other scholars

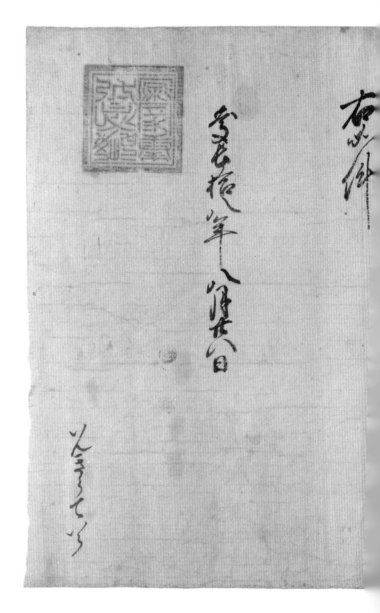

including Alexander Wylie, F. Max Müller, S.C. Malan,
and Sir Ernest Satow. Some hundred manuscripts,
including Narae hon (Nara picture books), were added
to the stock by donation or purchase in the early years
of the 20th century, when such material was more easily
available in Japan.

It was late in the 1950s when acquisition of Japanese
material was significantly increased and systematized.
For the next 30 years the acquisition policy was followed
fairly consistently: much emphasis was placed on the

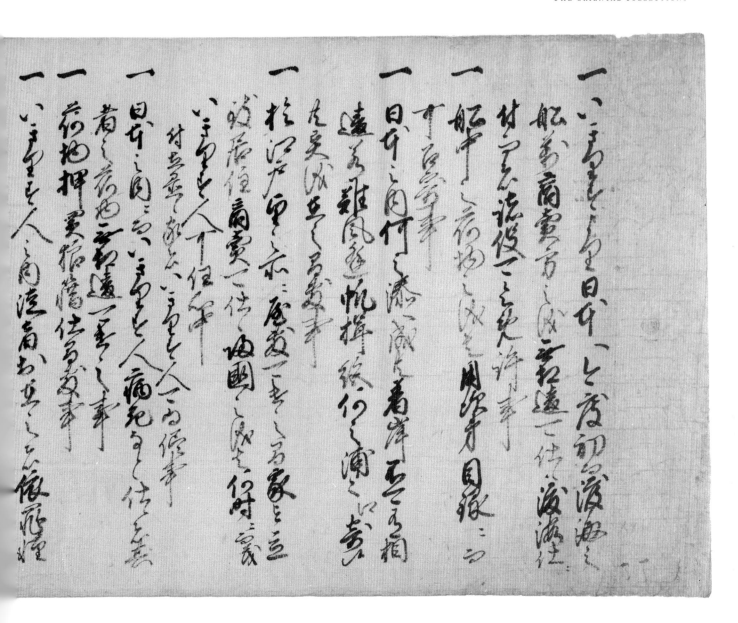

development of research collections in the humanities, reflecting the University's teaching and research programme. Since 1979 the scope of selection has been expanded, as research into the modern period has developed with the establishment of the Nissan Institute of Japanese Studies. The Library has undertaken to provide material in support of this new research interest, and has built up significant collection of works in the fields of modern history, politics, economics, and other social science studies.

In 1993, the Nissan Institute was built in the grounds of St. Antony's College, to which the Bodleian's extensive holdings on Japan were transferred. Combined with the residual collection of the Nissan Institute Library, the Bodleian Japanese Library was founded and opened to readers as the University's principal collection relating to Japan. The collection currently comprises some 78,000 volumes in Japanese together with over 18,000 volumes in European languages relating to Japan.

64 A late 18th-century manuscript of the *Rnying ma'i rgyud 'bum*

This Tibetan manuscript represents the first volume of a rare 33-volume set of *The Collected Tantras of the Ancients* (*Rnying ma'i rgyud 'bum*), a collection of texts from the oldest of the four major traditions of Tibetan Buddhism, the Rnying-ma school. It came to the Bodleian in 1909 under rather adventurous circumstances.

When in 1903 the Viceroy and Governor-General of India, Lord Curzon, ordered Major (later Sir) Francis E. Younghusband (1863–1942) to lead a British diplomatic mission to Tibet, no one could have imagined what impact this would have on the Tibetan holdings of various British institutions. This infamous British invasion of Tibet, retrospectively referred to as the 'Younghusband expedition', had initially aimed at negotiating trading rights and settling some outstanding border disputes. It soon turned into a military campaign, which reached the Tibetan capital Lhasa on 3 August 1904, leading to the signing of the Anglo-Tibetan Convention in the following month.

Among the members of this expedition was Lt.-Col. Lawrence A. Waddell (1854–1938), a former Professor of Chemistry and Pathology in the Calcutta Medical College and Assistant Sanitary Commissioner under the Government of India. Waddell had agreed to act as Chief Medical Officer to the expedition with a further commission to collect samples of Tibetan literature and religious art. A collection of nearly 2000 volumes of block prints and manuscripts 'amounting to over 300 mule loads of volumes' bore witness to the fact that, at least in his second task, he turned out to be successful. The circumstances of how and where Waddell obtained these texts remain obscure, but being in the company of British troops might have been an advantage. At times, however, his activities seem to have involved 'no little personal risk', for instance when more than once in the search for manuscripts, he 'had to run the gauntlet of exploding boxes of gunpowder'. On one occasion some texts with their wooden covers even seem to have saved his life

while he was caught in the battle of Gyantse, when they stopped a cannon ball from destroying his shelter.

Waddell's collection came to England in 1905 and was dispersed amongst the India Office Library and the British Museum in London, Cambridge University Library and the Bodleian. However, although the Bodleian received a share of more than 100 items, which entered the records as donations from the Government of India, this manuscript was not among them. Waddell had kept aside several items from the collection for his personal (financial) benefit. The Bodleian bought the present volume at Sotheby's on 17 March 1909. Twenty-nine volumes of the 33-volume set were given to the India Office Library (now part of the British Library), while the remaining three volumes (3, 9 and 31) are lost or in private hands.

The verso of the first leaf of the manuscript is covered by five layers of brocade, protecting three lines of text, written in gold lettering on black paper, and three miniatures. The latter are identified by inscriptions in the border underneath them. The central figure is the famous and highly revered Indian master Padmasambhava, who played a crucial role in the transmission of Indian Buddhism to Tibet during the 8th century, accompanied by his two consorts. On the left is the well known Tibetan scholar Kah-thog Rig-'dzin Tshe-dbang-nor-bu (1698–1755), on the right an Indian master.

Purchased, 1909. *MS Tibet a.24 (R), fol. 1v*

F. Younghusband, *India and Tibet: a history of the relations which have subsisted between the two countries from the time of Warren Hastings to 1910; with a particular account of the mission to Lhasa of 1904.* London, 1910.

L.A. Waddell, 'Tibetan manuscripts and books, etc., collected during the Younghusband Mission to Lhasa' in *Imperial and Asiatic Quarterly Review*, 34, 1912.

S. van Schaik, 'A catalogue of the first volume of the Waddell manuscript *rnying ma rgyud 'bum*' in *Tibet Journal*, 25 (1), 2000.

65 *Aṣṭasāhasrikāprajñāpāramitā*: the Perfection of wisdom in 8000 verses

This manuscript is one of only three that can be identified as having come from the great Buddhist monastic university of Nālandā in Bihar, India. It is dated in the colophon as being from the 15th year of the reign of Ramapala and, while opinion is divided as to the chronology of the Pala kings, this is generally thought to be between 1095 and 1099. It seems unlikely, on the basis of surviving evidence, that illustrations on palm-leaf manuscripts occur in India much before the year 1000, so this is an important survival from the very earliest period of this tradition. (Indian Buddhist manuscripts from this era owe their survival to having been taken to Nepal by monks fleeing the destruction of their monasteries by Turkish invaders in about 1200.) The wooden covers are of a later date than the manuscript and represent fine examples of 12th-century Nepalese painting. The *Aṣṭasā-hasrikāprajñāpāramitā* was one of a collection of 34 early Sanskrit manuscripts from the 11th to the 16th centuries purchased in 1900 from Dr. A.F.R. Hoernle. These were important additions to the Bodleian's Sanskrit manuscript collection, which, though extensive by the late 1800s, mainly consisted of 18th-century texts written on paper.

Illustrated Buddhist manuscripts were generally commissioned by pious laymen as a way of generating spiritual merit for themselves: the more beautiful a manuscript was, the greater the merit that came to the person who paid for its creation. The most favoured Buddhist text for illustration from this period was the *Prajñāpāramitā*, an abstruse metaphysical work on the nature of Buddhahood and wisdom. The treatise could be treated as an object of worship rather than a text

to be studied and the excellent condition of surviving illustrated palm leaf manuscripts of the work suggests that they were rarely read.

This manuscript is written in fine *Kuṭila* script and has a cycle of 18 miniatures illustrating scenes from the life of the Buddha and various Buddhist deities. On the first leaf the painting on the left has a deity holding a lotus with the moon on it. The centre image is of Buddha and the Hindu deity Indra. Buddhists dealt with deities of other religions by incorporating them into their system and giving them an inferior status to the Buddha. Thus Indra is depicted here as a disciple listening to the preaching of the Buddha. The picture on the right shows a deity holding a lotus with the sun on it. On the second leaf three scenes from Buddha's life are depicted. The miniature on the left shows Buddha seated under a Bo tree being presented with a bowl by two monkeys. This refers to the legend of the Monkey Tank, which recounts how monkeys built a pool at Vaisāli for the Buddha when he stayed there. The monkeys also took Buddha's alms-bowl up a tree, filled it with honey and presented it to him. The central miniature shows the Buddha in *Dharmacakra mudrā* (the mystic pose of teaching the law) under a Bodhi tree and the picture on the right shows the Buddha in *Parinirvāna* (death).

Purchased, 1900. *MS. Sansk. a. 7 (R), fols. 187v, 188r*

H.J. Stooke, 'An XI century illuminated palm leaf MS.' in *Oriental Art*, 1/1, (1948). *The world of Buddhism: Buddhist monks and nuns in society and culture*. Ed. by H. Becherts and R. Gombrich. London, Thames and Hudson, 1984.

66 *Hongxue yinyuan tuji* ('Traces of a wild swan in the snow'). Blockprinted edition, Yangzhou, 1849.

This is a fine printed edition from the magnificent collection of Sir Edmund Backhouse, which was given to the Library in stages between 1913 and 1922. The Backhouse Collection is a typical Chinese scholar's library—but a scholar of some substance—and provided Oxford with what at the time was one of the best Chinese rare book collections outside the Far East. Its large-scale editions more than quadrupled the Library's existing holdings of Chinese books, and it remains by far the greatest single donation of Chinese books in the Library's history. It is the only Chinese collection that bears the name of its donor.

This is the autobiography of the Manchu scholar-official Linqing, born in 1791 of a mother who was a poet and to whom he owed much of his literary talents and artistic inclinations. Linqing served in a number of capacities during his official career, among them director-general of river conservancy in Huaian in Jiangsu Province from 1833 to 1842, when he helped to strengthen the defences along the northern bank of the Yangtze River during the Anglo-Chinese Opium War. Later, he wrote an illustrated book on river conservancy. He retired to Peking in 1843, where he bought a property which he re-named Banmuyuan, the 'Half-acre Garden', whose delights he was only able to enjoy for a short time before his death in 1846.

The autobiography is written as a series of episodes,

each with a large folding illustration, and consists of three sections, each divided into two parts. It is printed on good quality white paper and bound in gold-flecked indigo covers, and is considered to be one of the finest examples of its period of the art of Chinese woodcut, a conservative and largely monochrome tradition, in which the subject is usually depicted using nothing more than line. The edition is not particularly rare, but is both valuable as an object and important as a text.

The illustration shows Linqing paying a visit to the Huangshicheng, the 'imperial archive' in Peking, in order to consult some government records. The Huangshicheng is a remarkable building which is still standing, and is situated to the south of the Forbidden City. It is built entirely of brick and stone as a protection against fire, and was used to house the *shilu* ('veritable records') and other documents of the imperial administration. These were contained in huge camphorwood boxes encased in gilded bronze with dragon reliefs, which are still in place, although their contents have been moved elsewhere. The picture shows one of these boxes opened, with an attendant bringing its contents for Linqing to examine on a table set up in the open air for the purpose. This picture together with others in the autobiography provide most valuable and interesting evidence of how libraries functioned in traditional China.

Presented, between 1913 and 1922. Backhouse 139

Modern political papers

67-72

The development of the modern political collections
has been one of the key aspects in the growth of the
Library's holdings of modern manuscript material during
the last fifty, and more particularly, the last thirty years.
Drawn mainly from the private papers of politicians,
public servants, journalists, broadcasters and others
active in public life from the 1840s to the present day it
numbers among its holdings the private papers of six
Prime Ministers—Benjamin Disraeli, H.H. Asquith,
Clement Attlee, Harold Macmillan, Harold Wilson
and James Callaghan; over fifty other mainly cabinet-
rank politicians; and over thirty civil servants (chiefly
diplomats). These are the private papers of the men
(and the exceptional women of their times) who helped
to shape the course of British history during the last
160 years. It is an international collection not only in
the range of themes covered but in the nationalities
of the correspondents and large numbers of overseas
correspondents. Six manuscripts have been selected
to illustrate aspects of the holdings' strengths: reform,
especially women's suffrage, and war are two of the key
themes covered, while the personal correspondence and
diaries of ministers and their wives often provide not only
insights into the individual's personality but ringside seats
at both key and everyday moments in British politics.
The British practice of ennobling public figures means
that most of the individuals featured here had titles, but
the collection's range stretches beyond the 'Great and
the Good' to encompass the papers of relatively minor
figures and the unsung men and women whose life stories
contributed to modern history. It is this mix which makes
the Bodleian holdings such a valuable historical resource.

67 Kimberley Papers

The purchase of the papers of John Wodehouse, 1st Earl
of Kimberley (1826–1902) in 1991 (with the assistance of
various grants) brought one of the last great 19th-century
collections remaining in private hands into the public
domain. A member of every Liberal cabinet from 1868
until the end of the century, Kimberley held a number
of key posts: serving as Lord Lieutenant of Ireland from
1864–66, Secretary of State for the Colonies, 1870–74
and 1880–82, for India, 1882–86 and 1892–94, and for
Foreign Affairs, 1894–95, making him well placed to
record contemporary events and personalities in the
nine volumes of his diaries starting in 1862 and ending
in 1901. Ireland, India, colonial and foreign policy are all
major themes in the Bodleian's modern political papers;
the acquisition of Lord Kimberley's papers enhanced the
coverage of these subjects taking the record forward from
the years documented in the papers of Lord Clarendon
(1800–70), who had held two of the same offices as
Kimberley—Lord Lieutenant of Ireland and Foreign
Secretary— just as the acquisition of Lord Morley's
papers nine years later in 2000 (item 68) would carry the
themes into the early 20th century.

This extract describes Prime Minister Gladstone's
final cabinet on 2 March 1894. The growing divisions
within the Liberal Party alluded to by Kimberley and
the rivalry between Rosebery, leader of the party in the
House of Lords, and Harcourt, leader in the House
of Commons, made the division of the leadership
unworkable. Rosebery resigned in 1896 and Harcourt
(whose papers are also in the Bodleian), in 1898.

Purchased, 1991. *MS. Eng. e.2793, fols. 201v–202r*

391   1894

It seems to be the prevailing
wish that we should come
to some understanding amongst
ourselves as to the future.
All agree in determination
to continue the Gt. if possible,
but I suppose so we. but for Salisbury?

Wednesday   Feb 28
Amusing to read the evidently
inspired article on Mr G.
in the 'Daily News'. Rosebery
is clearly first favourite, with
Harcourt to lead Commons.
Will they be able to agree?
Harcourt blusters now loudly,
but if R. is firm he will more
sure give way. Will R.
insist? That is the question.
I think he can hardly shrink
when it really comes to the point,
whatever he may say now,—
but he is a 'Sphynx' whom no
one can interpret.

1894   392
                                202
To night Salisbury rather
to the surprise of many
tho' I rather expected it,
moved & carried two
amendments on the L.G. Bill
He evidently is encouraged
by the impending resignation
of Mr G.
Thursday   March 2—
Last Cabinet of Mr G's
Govt.— We agreed not to
continue the contest with
the Lords. It is all essential
to terminate the existing
ministerial crisis as
soon as possible. At the
        at the request of my colleagues
end of the Cabinet I said
a few words of farewell
to Mr G. but quite broke
down. Harcourt fol-
lowed, reading a long
pompous letter which

153

68   Morley Papers

John (later Viscount) Morley (1838–1923) had more than
one distinguished career. Trained (but never practising)
as a barrister Morley started as a freelance journalist and
writer, becoming editor in 1867 of the recently launched
Fortnightly Review and a regular contributor throughout
the fifteen years of his editorship. His political career
began in 1883 and carried him to membership of
successive Liberal Cabinets under the premierships of
Gladstone, Campbell-Bannerman and H.H. Asquith,
serving twice as Chief Secretary of Ireland in 1886 and
1892–95, and as Secretary of State for India from 1905
to 1910. Morley was Lord President of the Council
when he wrote the draft memorandum shown here.
The document, written in August 1914, was intended
for posthumous publication, and as *Memorandum on
Resignation* was released in 1923 with a foreword by his
nephew, Guy Morley, and an introduction by Morley's
biographer, F.J. Hirst. This extract describes the divisive
impact of the declaration of the war against Germany on
4 August 1914, which caused Morley's resignation.

The range and depth of the collection is remarkable. Morley's general correspondence covers nearly
sixty years of British political life from 1865 to 1921, and
features many of the major figures of the day, including
one of the ministers mentioned in the memorandum,
Lord Beauchamp, and, from across the political divide,
Lord Curzon. A large part of the archive is concerned
with Ireland. Among the most intriguing aspects of the
collection is the discovery of the letters of Sir William
Harcourt lent by his son Lewis when Morley was
engaged on his mammoth task of writing the biography
of Gladstone, published in 1903. The long suspected
fate of these letters, missing since then from the
Harcourt papers (a collection deposited in the Library
several years ago), is now established. Morley's political,
literary and family correspondence is complemented by
a run of *Letts* diaries and a number of diary notebooks.

Acquired, 2000. *MS. Eng. d.3585, fols. 17–18*

17

The P.M. then drew himself together in his chair (next to mine), and opened with ~~~~ serious gravity of tone and aspect:— "I have to tell the Cabinet that I have this morning the resignations of five of its members in my hand: Bruce you all heard last night. To-day I have heard to the same effect from the senior of us all, the one who is the greatest source of the moral authority of the Govmt, de la Besides these two, we are to lose Sturm & Beauchamp. I understand further that many others in the Cabinet, perhaps a majority, share their views, though not at present following the same course. Then it is represented to me that a majority of our party in the H. of L. lean pretty strongly in the same direction. Well of the case? In which the country is placed, were of an ordinary kind, my course would be perfectly clear. I should go at once to the King and beg him to seek other Ministers. But the actual situation is far from ordinary, and I cannot persuade myself that the other party is led by men, or contains men, capable of dealing with it. Well, then

18

the idea of a Coalition naturally occurs to one. But Coalitions have hardly ever turned out well in our history. I could not look hopefully forward to that course. You [or WE] might shape a partial coalition. At any rate it is my duty to place my [or the] position plainly before the Cabinet."

~~Bruce was not present~~ They looked as if they expected me to say something. Naturally and most sincerely I expressed my regret at adding to the embarrassments of the hour, and repeated the points made in my letter of last morning. ~~I could only~~ What could I look forward to? unbesting wrestles with Austria (at whom I looked with personal benignity;) and should not being able to contribute a single useful hour. If I stayed, agreed to, I should be like the Publius, who withdrew from Paris for 2 or 3 days after joining! I feared I must beg the P.M. to let me write to my letter. Sturm followed; briefly but with much emotion, quivering lips and tears in his eyes. It was even firmer than these motions. Beauchamp said that he felt bound to associate himself with me. L.G. earnestly expostulated, especially with me. To my address.

69 Crampton Papers

Captain R.B. Hawley(1821–1898) made 80 or more pencil drawings during the Crimean War to illustrate his letters to Adelaide Jephson, sister of the diplomat Sir John Crampton. Other scenes depicted by Hawley, then in his mid-thirties, include 'The sick wharf', presumably a field station, in July 1855, a smiling fusilier with a stick slung over his shoulder from which dangles a dead bird (dinner?) and a soldier's grave at Green Hill, marked by a discarded cannon. Although the drawings are the most visually interesting aspect of the Crampton papers, they form only a small part of this collection which was donated in 1967. It fills 94 boxes and includes a considerable amount of correspondence relating to Anglo-American relations in the middle of the 19th century, including, in a link back to the Crimean material, the recruiting of Americans to fight in the British army in Russia. Other correspondence to survive (sadly very little remains for the last 20 years of Sir John Crampton's long life—born in 1805 he died in 1886) chronicles his postings to Hanover, Ireland, St. Petersburg and Madrid between the late 1850s and late 1860s. Private letters from Lord Clarendon, the Foreign Secretary, between 1852 and 1864 are unaccounted for (a fate shared by those from Lord Malmesbury and Lord John Russell) but this is offset to an extent by the long run of correspondence with Clarendon between 1853 and 1870 which survives in the latter's papers. Many of the Bodleian's modern political collections include interesting, even quirky, items, but the Hawley drawings outshine many and certainly the 'Feathers for tying flies sent from Bogata in 1857 by Philip Griffiths', also found among Crampton's papers.

Presented, 1967. *MS. Crampton 90/1, fols. 11,12*

'Arrival of the
Mail from Home.' 29 April/55.

Camp. April 26

Hyoscyamus Aureus

I wanted to draw the Postman here
but I can't give him a sufficiently
cheerful look — that he always has
when the mail comes in —

golden flowered Henbane.

Fresh Bread, Good Walnut —
Good Walnut —

70 Lady Selborne Papers

Maud, Countess of Selborne (d. 1950) was a remarkable woman of her time. Born into one of the great political dynasties, Lady (Beatrix) Maud Cecil married the 2nd Earl of Selborne in 1883. Unlike many political wives of her generation, however, Lady Selborne did not limit her political activity to supporting her husband's career, but, like Lady Jenny Churchill, Viscountess Castlereagh, Betty Balfour and others, actively campaigned for women's right to vote. Frustrated by the dominance of the 'antis' within the Primrose League—an organization dedicated to winning voters for the Conservative and Unionist Party (as it was then known)—she founded the Conservative and Women's Suffrage Association in 1908. Less militant than her correspondent's sister Lady Constance Lytton, she and a number of other

Conservative suffragists preferred to lobby personally to win support for the (ultimately defeated) Conciliation Bill, which would have extended the vote, but only to women householders. A small group of Lady Selborne's papers came into the Library as part of the donation of her husband's papers in 1970 followed, in 1979, by several more boxes of material when the additional papers of her son were donated. This letter is from the later acquisition, and in it Lord Lytton reports a conversation with Churchill, then First Lord of the Admiralty, about the latter's decision to resign from government in the event of the women's suffrage amendment being carried, and the effect this would have on Asquith's willingness to stand by his pledge on behalf of the government.

Presented, 1979. *MS. Eng. misc. c.686, fols. 3v–4r*

Woman suffrage Government".
"Well but your resignation would
not involve the fall of the whole
Government" I said, to wh he
replied "Oh but of course Asquith
wd resign also". I then tried
to convince him – I am afraid
with but little success – how
deeply dishonest such a course
wd be in view of the pledges
given by the Prime Minister &
often repeated in the clearest
possible words. 1) That if a
W.S. amendt were carried
the Govt as a whole wd accept
it 2/ that they wd proceed with the
bill through all its subsequent stages

& carry it into law. To make
such a pledge if he did not
mean to carry it out was
simply perjury!
Winston admitted that he cd
not speak for the P.M. & did
not know what his intentions
were but added that he cd not
conceive it possible that
Asquith wd do what he had
promised!
I said to Lady Willoughby that
if this sort of language were
being repeated in the lobby
it wd prove fatal to our
chances of carrying an amendt

71 Margot Asquith Papers

Margot Asquith, Countess of Oxford and Asquith (1864–1945) was an ardent supporter of her husband's politics. Highly intelligent and highly strung, Margot Asquith was well-known for her opulent life-style (she was a daughter of the Scottish millionaire industrialist, Sir Charles Tennant) and her directness, which risked alienating friends and acquaintances; but she could also be emotionally generous. Margot wrote as she spoke— with tremendous feeling—infusing her diaries and letters with immediacy and vitality. After Asquith lost office as Prime Minister in December 1916 Margot's output as a writer became prolific, producing volumes of both autobiography and biography and numerous magazine articles to provide an income. Aside from the diaries and literary papers, Margot Asquith's archive includes an excellent run of correspondence with many of the

age's leading figures and much family material, including letters from her beloved sister, Laura Lyttelton, who died in childbirth, Margot's two children, Princess Elizabeth Bibesco and the film director Anthony Asquith, her step-son, Raymond Asquith, and a small amount of Asquith's personal correspondence which survived his weeding of his own papers (the bulk of his papers, given in 1964, are overwhelmingly official). Lady Violet Bonham Carter's papers have recently taken their place alongside those of her father and step-mother.

In this letter, written on the morning of Violet's wedding to Maurice Bonham Carter, Margot shares her feelings about her step-daughter and her future husband, Bongy, with Asquith.

Presented, 1998. *MS. Eng. d.3314, fols. 38v–39r*

39

c'd be bitter as she w'd
give her her blessing —
She will not without
Yours but just forgive
her the mistakes I have
made. Violet is really
happy & ready to
marry soon while
people are still well
enough off to live
her beautiful presents
She. I have been

Rousseau-ing together.
She was in calm but
perfect spirits — as she
told her Bess is like
the King's daughter
all glorious within
& this is uncommon.
Elizabeth Puffin &
& I love him — so
does Cys —
If I have not
been a perfect
step-mother I will
be a perfect mother

72 Harold Macmillan and the Lady Waverley Papers

'Moreover, an ageing P.M. sh^d. not be like a beech tree (under which nothing grows) but like an oak (in whose shade all sorts of flowers, plants, & young shoots flourish)[.] In this respect, Lloyd George was better than Churchill.'

With the arrival of the vast archive of Harold Macmillan, 1st Earl of Stockton (1894–1986) on long term deposit in 1994 the Library's holdings of his correspondence were enormously strengthened. To develop the holdings further the Bodleian took an active interest in acquiring letters written by Macmillan, but the purchase of his letters to Ava, Lady Waverley (1896–1974) also alerted the Library to the historical significance of the Lady Waverley material.

Over the last few years the Library has purchased various small groups of Lady Waverley's papers: sometimes no more than a visitor's book, a few letters, occasionally larger amounts of correspondence, and most recently a run of letters from the leading thinker Sir Isaiah Berlin and some papers of her second husband, Viscount Waverley—the war-time Home Secretary Sir John Anderson (1882–1958) whom she married in 1941. (Her first husband, the gifted Foreign Office official, Ralph Wigram died in 1936). This letter is part of the first purchase, a sequence of letters from Harold Macmillan written between 1947 and 1974. In this case the letters are particularly interesting because they show Macmillan as a witty, caring, old friend who, in later life, often drew on their common interest in political life to amuse and support her through her serious illnesses and increasing infirmity. But in other batches of material Lady Waverley's reflections on her life, jotted down on scraps of paper and old notepads, show that she too would have been an excellent memoirist.

Purchased, 1993. *MS. Eng. c.4778, fols. 108,109*